CROCHET BASICS

CROCHET PROJECTS

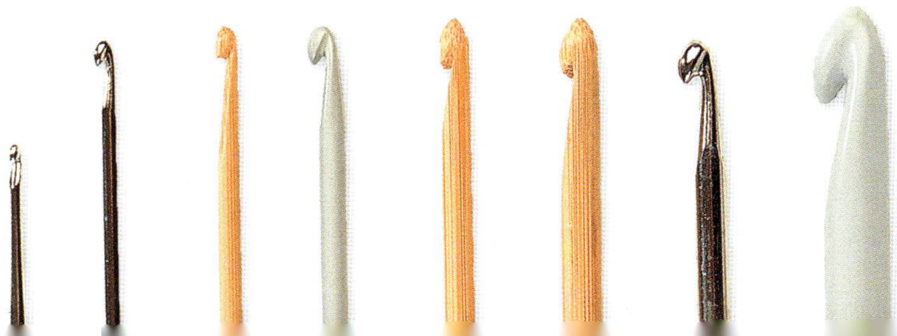

Welcome!

Knitting and crochet are two things I wish I had more time for in my schedule. There are so many beautiful garments you can make! When I was little, I would love watching my mom while she crocheted. It was fascinating to watch how row after row would magically turn into something special. I still have many of those pieces from my mom, along with an appreciation for the care and time it took to make them.

This special issue of DO features knitting and crochet projects you will want to make and wear! Many are on a beginner level, so they are great starter projects. But even if you are a seasoned needlecrafter, you will find yourself wanting to make some of these classically beautiful pieces. Compiled from the works of some of our favorite authors, there are sweaters to help you transition to spring (page 18), cute accessories (page 40), and special occasion pieces to make for a night on the town (page 78).

If you are new to knitting or crochet, we've also included the basic stitches and techniques you'll need to get started. You'll notice that each of our contributors has a different approach to how they teach a project (some will need to be converted to American equivalents), and that you may not be able to find an exact yarn used, but regardless of how you get there, we know you will be pleased with your results.

Happy Needlework!

Melissa Younger

DO magazine PRESENTS knitting & CROCHET PROJECTS

Design Originals Presents Knitting & Crochet Projects
Spring 2018, Volume 4, number 1, issue 11
ISSN 2572-0848

Design Originals: DO Magazine
903 Square Street, Mount Joy, PA 17552
Phone: 717-560-4703 | Fax: 717-560-4702

PUBLISHER Alan Giagnocavo
VICE PRESIDENT–CONTENT Christopher Reggio
MANAGING EDITOR Melissa Younger
CONTRIBUTORS Melody Griffiths, Hilary Mackin, Val Pierce, Sue Whiting
EDITORIAL STAFF Colleen Dorsey, Kaitlyn Ocasio, Llara Pazdan, Laura Taylor
LAYOUT AND DESIGN STAFF Wendy Reynolds

Newsstand Distribution: Curtis Circulation Company
Circulation Consultant: National Publisher Services
Printed in USA.

Pages 4–10 content from Hilary Mackin's *Simple Stylish Knits*
Images from pages 1 (bottom) and 50 and content from pages 50–56 from Melody Griffiths's *Simple Stylish Crochet*

Shutterstock photos: Africa Studio (2, 51); Immensus (3); Nataliia Pyzhova (5 bottom); JeniFoto (9 bottom); Kostikova Natalia (10 top, 94 top); Semiletava Hanna (black and white illustration on inner front cover, 16 bottom, 22 bottom right, 24, 38 bottom left, 42 bottom, 48 bottom, 72 bottom); Shcherbakova Natalia (49); normallens (54 bottom); Yana Radaeva (56 bottom); Talirina (black and white illustrations on 12, 26, 28 right, 29 bottom right, 32 right, 34 top, 38 top, 40, 42 top, 48 top right, 58, 62 bottom, 68, 78, 82, 86, 88)

Knitting basics

Basic Information

EQUIPMENT

Knitting requires very little equipment - all you really need is a pair of needles and some yarn and you are ready to go. However, there are many different types of yarn available now and a whole range of needles to choose from, as well as some other equipment that you will find useful.

NEEDLES

Knitting needles are available in aluminum, plastic, and wood, although the larger sizes are only made in plastic and wood, as they are lighter and easier to hold.

Standard needle sizes range from 2 mm to 10 mm, although you will also find fat needles that are up to 1 in. (25 mm). Generally, thick yarns are knitted using large needles and thinner yarns with small ones. The thicker the needle, the larger the stitch and the more quickly your work will progress. Needles also come in different lengths - choose ones which you find most comfortable to work with.

Cable needles are short needles which are pointed at both ends. They are used for moving stitches from one position to another when working cables.

Circular needles have two short needles which are each pointed and joined by a piece of flexible nylon that varies in length. They are much easier to handle than four double-pointed needles and are useful for neckbands or when picking up a large number of stitches around a front edge. They are ideal for any work which may be difficult to fit on a conventional needle.

OTHER KNITTING ESSENTIALS

CROCHET HOOKS

These are very useful for picking up dropped stitches and working edgings on finished garments, as well as for casting off, joining seams, and adding tassels.

STITCH HOLDER

This keeps stitches that you are not using in place until you need them. You could also use a spare needle for this.

TAPESTRY NEEDLES

Blunt-ended needles with large eyes are used for sewing up items as sharp needles may split the yarn and weaken it.

TAPE MEASURE

Use a good tape measure - ideally one that doesn't stretch, as accurate measurements are important when checking gauge.

SCISSORS

Have a sharp pair on hand for cutting lengths of yarn.

ROW COUNTER

This helps you keep track of stitches and rows completed.

PINS

Use long pins with large heads when pinning pieces together so that they will not get lost in the knitting.

KNITTING NEEDLE CONVERSION TABLE

METRIC	AMERICAN	BRITISH
2 mm	00	14
2¼ mm	1	13
2¾ mm	2	12
3 mm	2/3	11
3¼ mm	3	10
3¾ mm	5	9
4 mm	6	8
4½ mm	7	7
5 mm	8	6
5½ mm	8	5
6 mm	9	4
6½ mm	10	3
7 mm	10½	2
7½ mm	11	1
8 mm	12	0
9 mm	13	00
10 mm	15	000

YARNS

There is currently a huge selection of yarns available, and choosing the right one can be daunting. You will find both natural and synthetic yarns as well as some synthetic mix yarns. Natural yarns such as wool and cotton are more expensive but they are often easier to work with. Synthetic yarns tend to be stronger.

Wool is easily available, long lasting, and very warm. Merino sheep have the most abundant and highest quality yarn.

Cotton is strong, non-allergenic, and easy to wash but is less elastic than wool.

Mohair yarn comes from Angora goats. The long silky fibers make it very warm.

Angora is like mohair, but softer. It is made from the hair of the Angora goat or rabbit.

Alpaca is less fluffy than mohair and angora; it is made from the hair of a llama-like animal.

Cashmere is the most expensive and luxurious of yarns, made from the fine downy hair of a special breed of goat.

Chenille is a velvety yarn made of tufts of cotton and synthetic yarn.

CHOOSING YARNS

All the patterns specify which yarns have been used. To ensure the item appears the same as in the pattern, you should use the yarn that the pattern recommends. If you cannot find the same yarn, choose one of a similar weight and type, and knit a sample to check the gauge and appearance. When buying yarn, check the ball band for the dye lot number and make sure you buy balls with the same number.

GETTING STARTED

GARTER STITCH

This is the simplest of all knitted stitches and is formed by working every row in the same stitch, either knit or purl, forming the same pebbly pattern on the front and the back making it reversible. It has a sideways stretch. If every row is purled, however, you do not produce such a firm fabric.

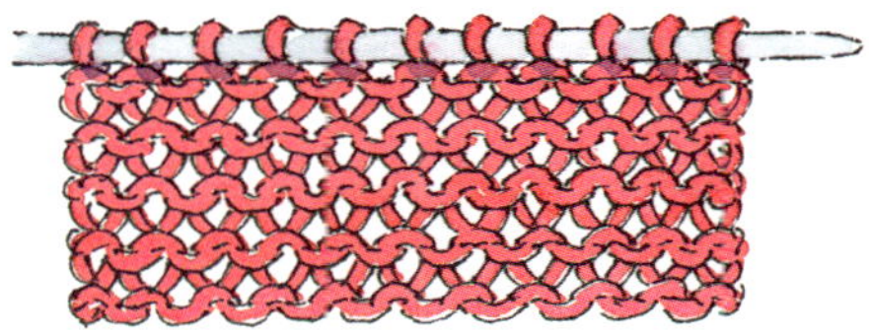

STOCKING STITCH

This is the smoothest of all knitted stitches and is stretchy horizontally. It is formed by working alternate rows of knitted stitches and purled stitches. The smooth, knitted side is usually called the right side. When the pattern uses the purl side as the right side, it is referred to as reverse stocking stitch.

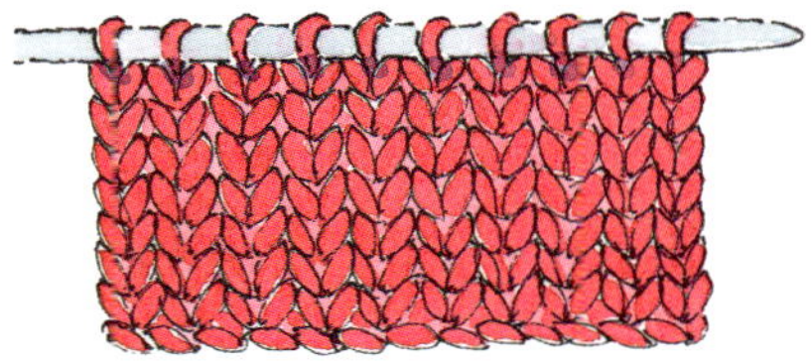

MOSS STITCH

This stitch forms a firmer fabric than stocking stitch and is created by alternately working knit and purl stitches. Stitches that are knitted on one row will be knitted on the next row, and stitches that are purled on one row will be purled on the next row. For an odd number of stitches, the instructions will be as follows;
K1, *p1, k1, rep from * to end. Repeat this row.

As this stitch does not curl at the edges, it is ideal for edges. It is also reversible.

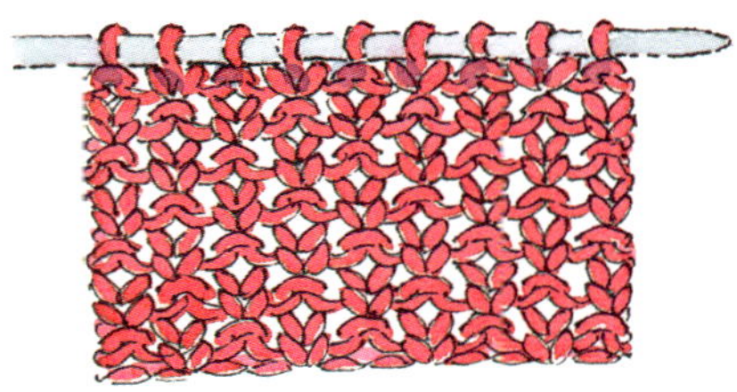

RIB STITCH

This is formed by alternating knit and purl stitches across the same row. The knitted chain stitch forms a rib and the fabric shrinks inward and has a strong sideways stretch. It is particularly suitable for cuffs and necks and body edges to form a neat, stretchable finish. It is usually worked on smaller needles than were used for the main body of the garment.

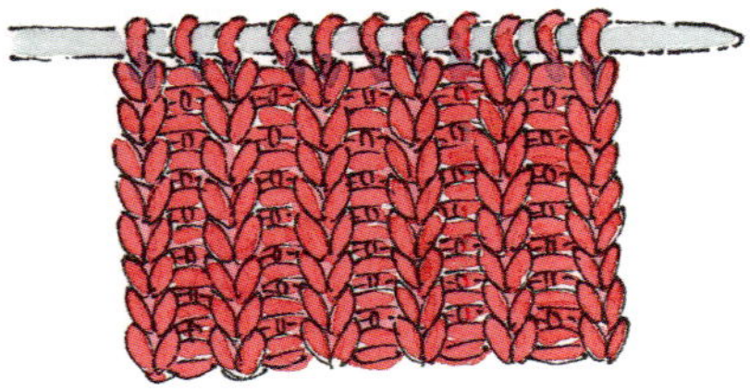

GAUGE

Making sure you have the correct gauge is extremely important as it controls the shape and size of the knitted item. To make a gauge swatch, knit a sample square slightly larger than 4 in. (10 cm) using the same yarn, needles, and stitch pattern stated in the pattern. Smooth out the sample on a flat surface, being careful not to stretch it. Using long pins, mark out the gauge measurement given in the pattern, usually 4 in. (10 cm). To determine the stitch gauge of the knitting, count the number of stitches between the pins. Remember to include any half stitches over the width of a garment; a half stitch left uncalculated may amount to several inches/centimeters in the final width.

To determine the length of the knitting, measure the number of rows. Place a rigid ruler or tape vertically along the fabric and count the number of rows to the inch/centimeter. If the number of stitches given in the pattern knit up too wide, it means the knitting is too loose and a size smaller needle should be used. If too small, then the knitting is too tight and a larger needle should be used.

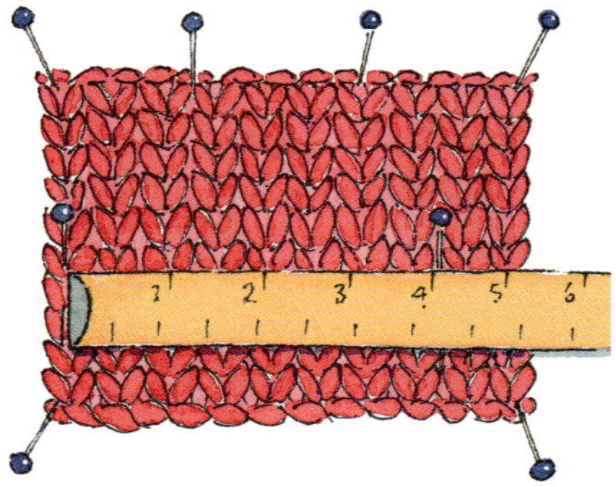

FOLLOWING A PATTERN

Knitting patterns are written in a language all of their own. Before starting to knit any pattern, always read it through so you are familiar with the terms.

Abbreviations are used for many of the repetitive words that occur in the instructions. Any additional abbreviations will be given with each individual pattern.

Asterisks are used to indicate repetition of a sequence of stitches. For example: *k3, p1, rep from * to end. This means knit 3 stitches and purl 1 stitch to the end of the row.

Brackets are used where a set of instructions need to be worked a number of times. For example: [k3, p1] 4 times. This means that the stitches within the brackets are worked 4 times in total. Brackets are also used where instructions are given for multiple sizes; in the patterns figures are given for the smallest size first and the larger sizes follow in brackets. Where the figure "0" appears in a set of brackets, no stitches or rows are to be worked in that particular size.

The instruction "alt" usually occurs during an instruction for shaping, for example: increase 1 stitch at the end of next and every alt row until there are 10 sts. This means that, counting the next row as row 1, the increase is worked on rows 1, 3, 5, 7, etc. until the required number of stitches is reached. If the instruction reads "increase 1 stitch at end of every alt row," then the increases are worked on rows 2, 4, 6, 8, etc.

CARE OF YARNS AND GARMENTS

The correct after-care of all knitted garments is extremely important if they are to retain their original texture and shape. Many of the yarns available today are machine-washable and the ball band will clearly indicate where this is applicable. If in any doubt, handwash in warm soapy water. Check the ball band to see whether the yarn can be dry cleaned.

When washing by hand, handle the knitting carefully and never lift the garment by the shoulders as the weight of the wet wool will drag the knitting out of shape. Squeeze out excess moisture gently without wringing. Support the overall weight with both hands and rinse thoroughly before drying to avoid matting. Spin dry for a short time only.

Never tumble dry a knitted garment. Knitting should be dried away from direct heat and laid out flat on a suitable surface. Spread the knitting out gently on a towel, and smooth out any creases. Leave until completely dry and then place over a line for final airing.

ABBREVIATIONS	
alt – alternate	rem – remain(ing)
beg – beginning	rep – repeat
cont – continue	RH – right-hand
dec – decreas(e)(ing)	RS – right side
foll – following	sl 1 – slip one stitch
g st – garter stitch (every row knit)	sl1-k1-psso – slip one, knit one, pass slipped stitch over the knit one
inc – increas(e)(ing)	st(s) – stitch(es)
k – knit	st st – stocking stitch, (knit row is RS, purl row is WS)
k1b – knit one in back of loop	tbl – through back of loop(s)
k2tog – knit two stitches together	tog – together
LH – left-hand	WS – wrong side
M1 – make one by picking up loop which lies between st just worked and next st and working into the back of it	wyib – with yarn in back.
p – purl	wyif – with yarn in front
p1b – purl one in back of loop	yb – yarn back
p2tog – purl two stitches together	yf – yarn forward
patt – pattern	yo – yarn over needle
psso – pass slipped st over	yrn – yarn round needle
rem – remain(ing)	

Never hang knitting to drip dry. The weight of the wet fabric will pull the garment out of shape.

If a garment is properly dried, it should not need pressing. If it does, check the instructions on the ball band. Some yarns may need steaming or pressing over a damp cloth. Never use a heavy hand when pressing knitted garments as this could distort the shape badly, and never press ribbing.

Some yarns are prone to pilling during wear. This means that loose fibers gather into balls of fluff on the surface of the knitting. These can either be picked off, brushed, or combed away, or go over the surface with a strip of tape, sticky side down. Special implements can be bought for this purpose. If a snag occurs never cut it off; instead, take a blunt needle and push the snag through to the wrong side of the work. Gently tighten the yarn until the stitch is the right size and then knot the end on the wrong side.

BASIC TECHNIQUES

INCREASING AND DECREASING

Garments are most commonly shaped by increasing or decreasing the number of stitches in a row. There are many different ways of increasing and decreasing the number of stitches, and each will create a slightly different appearance.

Increases and decreases are usually worked in pairs at each end of the row on the symmetrical pieces (back, sleeves, etc.) to give a balanced shape.

YARN FORWARD INCREASE

To make the yarn forward increase in a knit row, bring the yarn to the front, take it over the right-hand needle, and knit the stitch. The complete increase creates a visible hole and is often used in lace patterns. The increase is abbreviated in knitting patterns as yf (yarn forward).

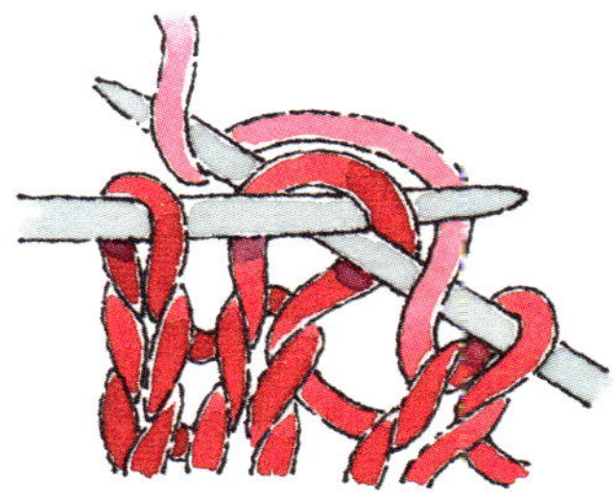

In a purl row, take the yarn over the right-hand needle to the back of the work, then under the needle to the front. The abbreviation is yrn (yarn round needle).

MAKE 1 INCREASE

Lift the yarn lying between the stitch just worked and the next stitch and place it on the left-hand needle, then knit (or purl) into the back of this loop. This increase is abbreviated as M1 (make 1).

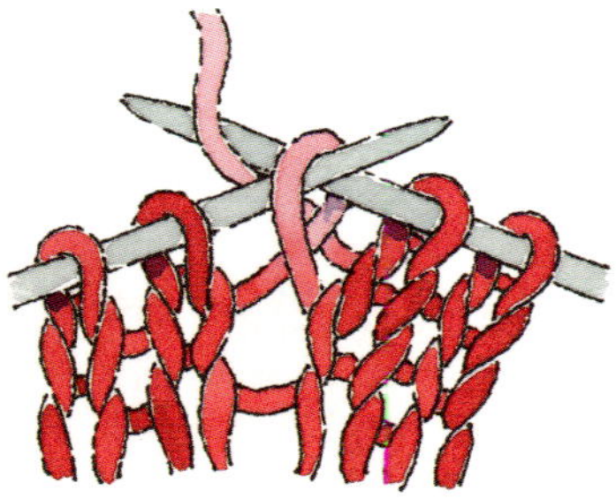

SLIP STITCH DECREASE

Slip the next stitch onto the right-hand needle without knitting it, then knit the next stitch. Lift the slipped stitch over the knitted stitch and drop it off the needle. This decrease is abbreviated as sl 1, k1, psso (on right side) and sl 1, p1, psso (on wrong side).

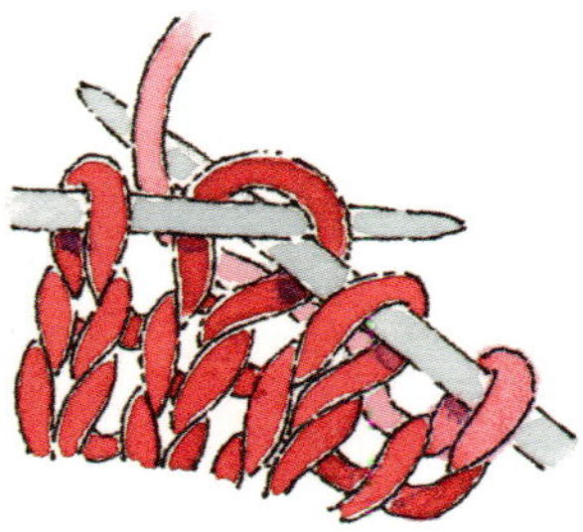

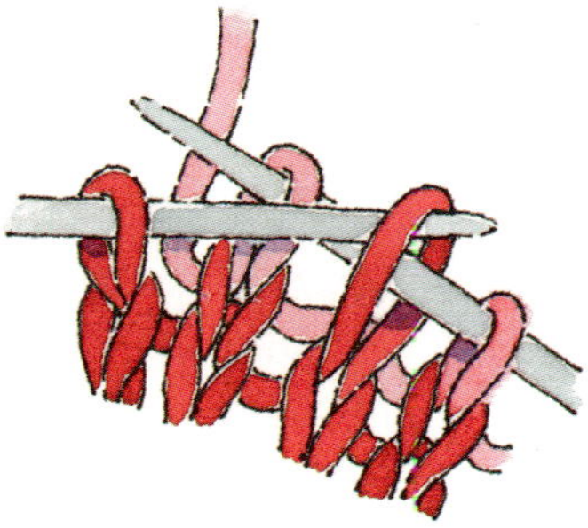

WORKING TWO STITCHES TOGETHER

This decrease is worked simply by inserting the right-hand needle through two stitches instead of one and then knitting them together as one stitch. On a purl row, insert the needle purlwise through the two stitches and purl in the usual way. This decrease is abbreviated as k2tog (right side) or p2tog (wrong side).

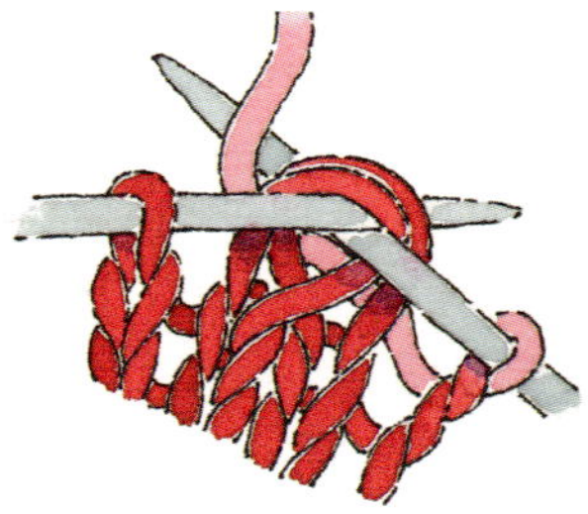

CHANGING COLOR

To join in a new color at the start of a row, insert the needle into the first stitch and, using the new color, make a loop over the right-hand needle. Pull through to complete the stitch and continue to the end of the row. Carry the yarn up the side of the work for narrow stripes but break it off and rejoin it for wider stripes.

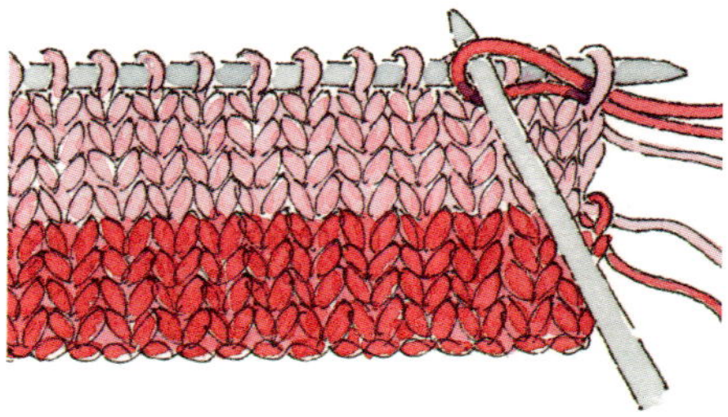

Where colors are worked in blocks, it is best to use a separate ball of yarn for each section. Twist the yarns over each other at the junction of each color change to avoid a hole forming. When the color change occurs in vertical lines, cross the yarns on both knit and purl rows. When the color change is on a slanting line, the yarns need to be crossed on alternate rows.

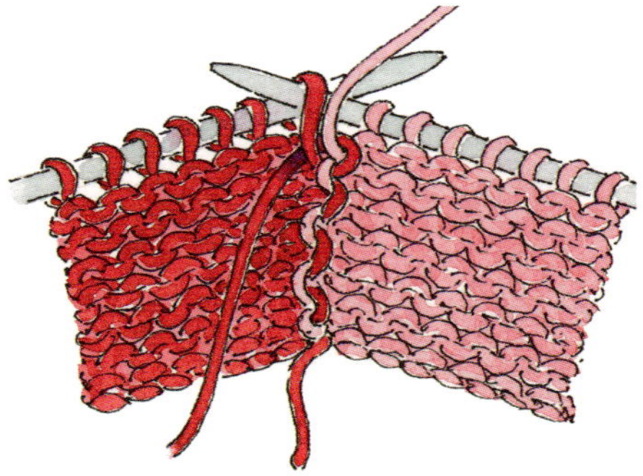

MAKING HORIZONTAL BUTTONHOLES

These may be worked on the main fabric or on a separate narrow band.

Work to the position of the buttonhole and cast off the number of stitches required for the width of the button and knit to the end of the row. Work to within one stitch of the cast-off stitches and knit twice into it. Then cast on one stitch less than was cast off and work to the end of the row.

Once the garment is complete, you can finish off the buttonhole by working round it in buttonhole stitch.

FINISHING GARMENTS

Even the simplest garments require neat and careful finishing, so it is worth spending some time at the final stages for professional looking garments.

Before you begin joining pieces together, weave in any loose ends of yarn into a seam edge. Cover the pieces with a damp cloth and press gently with a steam iron - this will make them easier to join.

JOINING SEAMS

There are various different ways of sewing knitted pieces together but most use the backstitch seam method. Use a blunt-ended needle. Place the pieces to be joined together with their right sides facing inward, ensuring that the stitches and rows are aligned. Sewing into the center of each stitch, bring the needle out one stitch in from the edge, insert the needle one stitch back, and bring the needle out one stitch ahead of the emerging thread. Sew a ¼ in. (a few mm) in from the edge of the knitting.

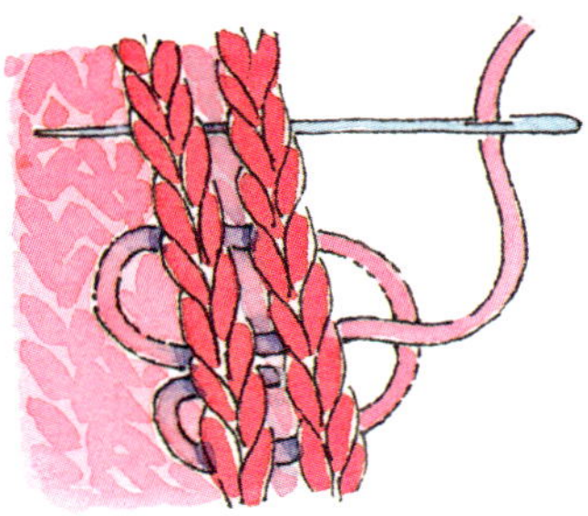

JOINING SLEEVES

The top of the sleeve and the armhole into which it is set can often be different shapes, so care needs to be taken when inserting the sleeves. Once the shoulder seams have been joined, fold the sleeve in half lengthwise. Mark the center of the top of the sleeve and the midway points between the center and the underarm with pins.

On the main body of the garment, mark the center of the shoulder join and midway points from that point and the underarm with pins. With right sides together, pin the sleeve into the armhole, matching up the marker pins. Using a backstitch seam, sew the sleeve seam on the inside.

COLLARS

Collars can either be knitted in by first picking up stitches around the neck edge or made separately and sewn on.

For a picked-up collar, join one shoulder as indicated on pattern. Divide the neck edge into sections and mark with pins to space the picked-up stitches evenly, then calculate how many stitches will be needed for each section. When working a non-reversible stitch such as stocking stitch, remember to pick up the stitches from the correct side to ensure that the pattern is on the right side when the collar is turned over.

For a sewn-on collar, divide the neck edge and the inner collar edge into the same number of equal sections and mark them with a pin. With the right side of the collar facing the wrong side of the garment, pin the two edges together and sew.

ZIPPERS

Always insert an open-ended zipper with the fastener closed to ensure that both sides match.

Pin the zipper in position, taking care not to stretch the knitting. Use an ordinary sewing needle and matching thread. With the right side of the work facing, sew in the zipper with a back-stitch seam keeping as close to the knitted edge as possible. Always work from top to bottom and take care not to cover the zipper teeth. Slip stitch down the zipper edges on the inside afterward.

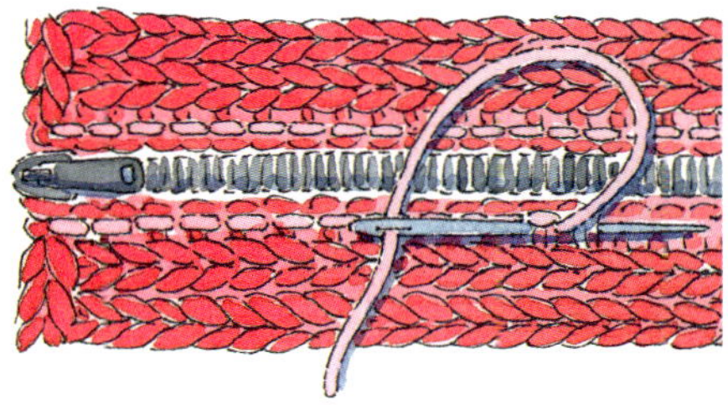

DECORATIVE EDGES

These may be used to trim garments. They can be made separately and sewn on afterward or knitted as part of the garment. Knit a length as indicated on the pattern, then with right side of edging to right side of garment, divide into equal sections and pin; sew in position using a back stitch. Allow extra ease for any curves on the main garment, so that the edging lies flat after sewing.

MAKING TASSELS

Cut out a piece of card the same length that you want the tassel to be. Wind yarn around the card to the required thickness. Thread a needle with yarn and pull it under the strands at the top of the card. Tie securely, leaving a long end. Using a sharp pair of scissors, cut through the yarn at the other end of the card. Wind the long end of yarn around the tassel several times about ¾ in. (1.5 cm) from the top, and secure by pushing the needle up through the middle of the tassel.

FRINGING

Cut the yarn into the required lengths - just over twice the required finished length of the fringe. Fold in half and, with the wrong side of the fabric facing you, draw a loop through the edge stitch using a crochet hook. Then draw the loose ends of the strands through this loop and pull down tightly to form a knot. Repeat at regular intervals.

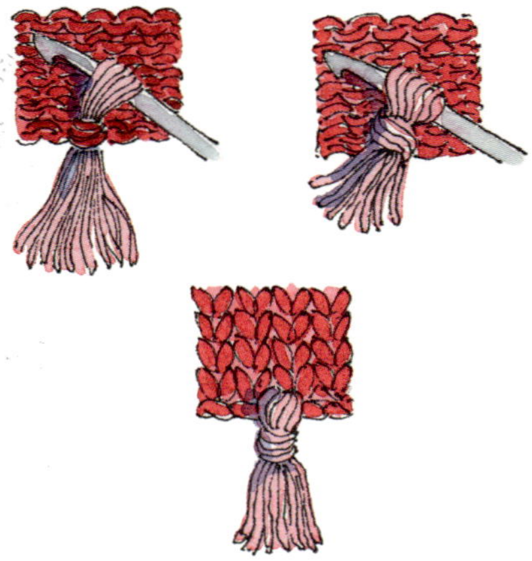

SEWN-ON POCKETS

Use a slip stitch seam to apply the pocket, taking care to keep the line of the pocket and main fabric straight.

A useful tip is to use a fine knitting needle, pointed at both ends, to pick up every alternate stitch along the line of the main fabric, then catch one stitch from the edge of the pocket and one stitch from the needle alternately. Make sure that the lower edge of the pocket lies in a straight line across a row of the main fabric.

ADAPTING PATTERNS

Sometimes it may be necessary to alter a pattern to suit your own body measurements. Working with the gauge quoted on the pattern, calculate the amendments necessary to the stitches and rows and mark the alterations on the pattern.

knitting PROJECTS

long shawl-collared coat

The interesting yarn, together with an easy slip stitch pattern, gives extra appeal to this long line coat, which is perfect for wearing over a pair of casual trousers for a warm yet elegant look.

By Hilary Mackin, from her book *Simple Stylish Knits*

BEGINNER

MEASUREMENTS

To fit bust

in.	32	34	36	38	40
cm	81	86	91	97	102

Actual width

in.	37½	39½	41	44½	46
cm	95	100	104	113	117

Actual length

in.	35½	35½	36¼	36¼	37
cm	90	90	92	92	94

Actual sleeve seam

18 in. (46 cm)

➤ In the instructions figures are given for the smallest size first; larger sizes follow in brackets. Where only one set of figures is given, this applies to all sizes.

MATERIALS

- 14 (14:15:15:16) x 100 g balls of Rowan Ribbon Twist in Ribble 111
- Pair of 12 mm needles
- Stitch holders
- 3 buttons

GAUGE

9 sts and 11 rows to 4 in. (10 cm) measured over pattern using 12 mm needles.

ABBREVIATIONS

See page 7.

COAT

BACK

With 12 mm needles cast on 51 (55:59:63:67) sts.

Foundation row: WS. *K3, p1; rep from * to last 3 sts, k3.

Row 1: *P3, k1 winding yarn twice around needle; rep from * to last 3 sts, p3.

Row 2: *K3, sl 1 purlwise wyif and dropping extra loop, yb; rep from * to last 3 sts, k3.

Rows 1 and 2 form the patt. Cont in patt dec 1 st at each end of the 17th and 5 (2:6:6:4) foll 8th (8th:6th:6th:6th) rows [39 (49:45:49:57) sts], then on the 0 (4:1:1:4) foll 0 (6th:4th:4th:4th) rows [39 (41:43:47:49) sts], then inc 1 st at each end of the next and foll 6th row. [43 (45:47:51:53) sts.]

Work 10 rows straight, ending with a WS row. [74 rows - work measures approximately 26½ in. (67 cm) from beg.]

SHAPE ARMHOLES

Cast off 2 (2:3:3:4) sts at beg of the next 2 rows [39 (41:41:45:45) sts], then dec 1 st at each end of the next 3 rows [33 (35:35:39:39) sts], then on the 2 foll alt rows [29 (31:31:35:35) sts]. Work a further 15 (15:17:17:19) patt rows, ending with a WS row.

SHAPE SHOULDERS AND BACK NECK

Cast off 4 (4:4:5:5) sts at beg of the next row, work in patt until there are 5 (6:6:6:6) sts on RH needle after cast-off, turn and leave rem sts on a st holder. Work on these sts for first side.

Dec 1 st at neck edge on the next row. Cast off rem 4 (5:5:5:5) sts.

With RS facing, cast off the center 11 (11:11:13:13) sts and work in patt to end. Complete this side to match first side, reversing shapings.

POCKET LININGS (make 2)

With 12 mm needles cast on 11 sts. Cont in st st beg with a knit row. Work 14 rows and leave on a st holder.

LEFT FRONT

With 12 mm needles cast on 30 (34:36:38:40) sts.

Cont in patt as follows:

Foundation row: WS. (P1, k1) 3 times, p1, k3 (3:5:3:5), p1, *k3, p1; rep from * to last 3 sts, k3.

Some experience is needed to do the shaping and collar on this garment.

The slip stitch pattern used to make this coat is very easy to work.

This coat requires neat finishing.

Row 1: *P3, k1 winding yarn twice around needle; rep from * to last 10 (10:12:10:12) sts, p3 (3:5:3:5), (k1, p1) 3 times, k1.

Row 2: (P1, k1) 3 times, p1, k3 (3:5:3:5), p1, *k3, sl 1 purlwise wyif and dropping extra loop, yb; rep from * to last 3 sts, k3.

Cont in patt as Back, dec 1 st at side edge on the 17th and 3 (2:4:4:4) foll 8th (8th:6th:6th:6th) rows [26 (31:31:33:35) sts], then on the 0 (2:0:0:1) foll 0 (6th:0:0:4th) rows [26 (29:31:33:34) sts]. Work 5 (1:5:5:1) rows, ending with WS row.

PLACE POCKET

Next row: Patt 0 (0:2:2:0) tog, patt 4 (5:4:5:8) sts, rib across next 11 sts for pocket top, turn and work 2 rows in rib on these 11 sts, cast off these 11 sts. Break yarn. With RS facing, rejoin yarn to one pocket lining, cont in patt across these sts then patt 4 (6:7:7:8), rib 7. [26 (29:30:32:34) sts.]

Work 1 (3:5:5:1) rows. Dec 1 st at side edge on the next and 1 (1:1:1:2) foll 8th (6th:4th:4th:4th) row [24 (27:28:30:31) sts], then inc 1 st at side edge on the next and foll 6th row. [26 (29:30:32:33) sts.]

Work 4 rows straight, ending with a WS row. Place marker at front edge on last row. ***

SHAPE NECK AND COLLAR

Row 1: Patt to last 10 sts, patt 3tog, M1, rib to end. [25 (28:29:31:32) sts.]

Row 2: Rib 8, patt to end.

Row 3: Patt to last 8 sts, M1, rib to end. [26 (29:30:32:33) sts.]

Row 4: Rib 9, patt to end.

Row 5: Patt to last 9 sts, M1, rib to end. [27 (30:31:33:34) sts.]

Row 6: Rib 10, patt to end.

SHAPE ARMHOLE

Row 7: Cast off 2 (2:3:3:4) sts at beg of the next row, patt to last 13 sts, patt 3tog, M1, rib to end. [24 (27:27:29:29) sts.]

Row 8: Rib 11, patt to end.

Row 9: Patt 2tog, patt to last 11 sts, M1, rib to end. [24 (27:27:29:29) sts.]

Row 10: Rib 12, patt to last 2 sts, patt 2tog.

Row 11: Patt 2tog, patt to last 12 sts, M1, rib to end. [23 (26:26:28:28) sts.]

Row 12: Rib 13, patt to end.

1st size

Row 13: Patt 2tog, patt to last 13 sts, M1, rib to end. [23 sts.]

Row 14: Rib 14, patt to end.

2nd, 3rd, 4th, and 5th sizes

Row 13: Patt 2tog, patt to last 16 sts, patt 3tog, M1, rib to end. [(24:24:26:26) sts.]

Row 14: Rib 14, patt to end.

All sizes

Row 15: Patt 2tog, patt to last 14 sts, M1, rib to end.

Rows 16, 18, and 20: In patt as set.

Row 17: Patt to last 15 sts, M1, rib to end.

Row 19: Patt to last 16 sts, M1, rib to end.

Row 21: Patt to last 17 sts, M1, rib to end. [26 (27:27:29:29) sts.]

3rd, 4th, and 5th sizes

Row 22: In patt as set.

Row 23: Patt to last 18 sts, M1, rib to end. [(28:30:30) sts.]

5th size

Row 24: In patt as set.

Row 25: Patt to last 19 sts, M1, rib to end. [31 sts.]

All sizes

Work 9 rows as set, ending at side edge. [26 (27:28:30:31) sts.]

SHAPE SHOULDER

Cast off 4 (4:4:5:5) sts at beg of the next row, cast off 4 (5:5:5:5) sts on the foll alt row.

[18 (18:19:20:21) sts.]

Next row: Rib 15 (15:16:17:18) sts, slip next st onto RH needle and take yarn to opposite side of work between needle, slip the same st back onto LH needle (referred to as wrap 1), turn.

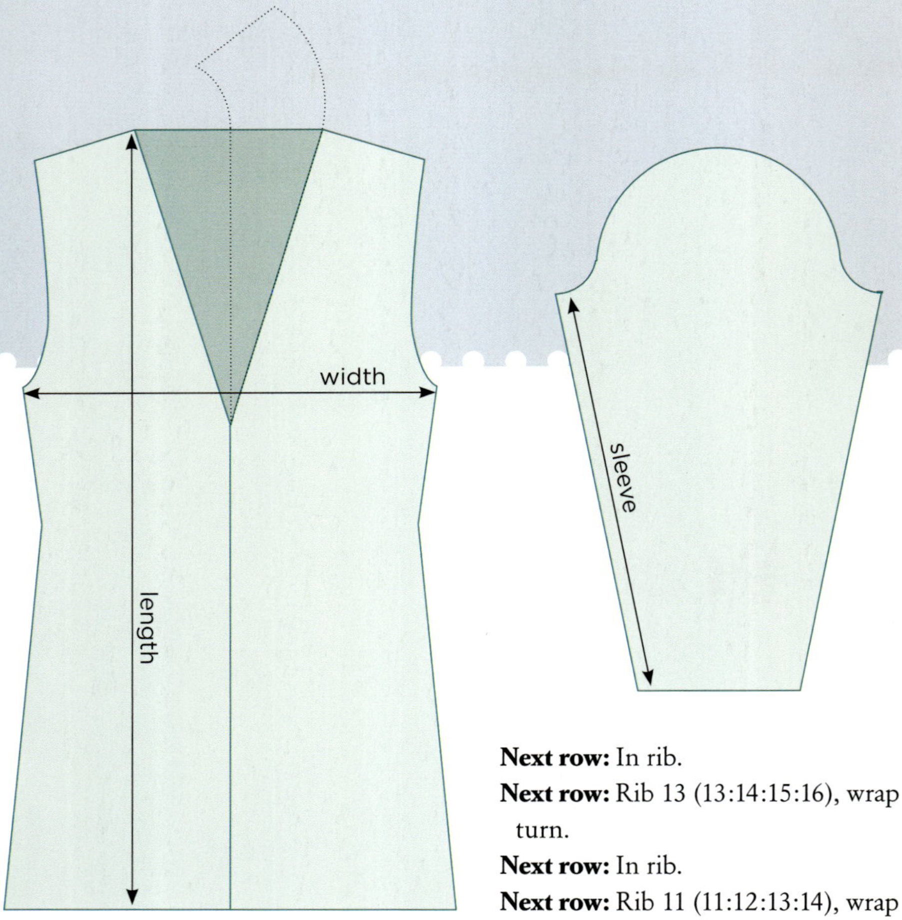

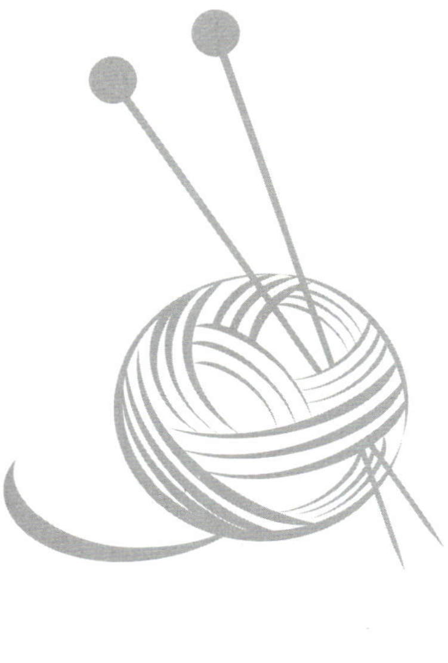

Next row: In rib.

Next row: Rib 13 (13:14:15:16), wrap 1, turn.

Next row: In rib.

Next row: Rib 11 (11:12:13:14), wrap 1, turn.

Cont without shaping until collar is of sufficient length to go halfway across back of neck, ending with a WS row. Cast off.

Mark the positions of 3 buttons, the first in line with cast-off edge on pocket top, the last 4 rows down from marker and the remainder spaced between.

RIGHT FRONT

With 12 mm needles cast on 30 (34:36:38:40) sts.

Cont in patt as follows:

Foundation row: *K3, p1; rep from * to last 10 (10:12:10:12) sts, k3 (3:5:3:5), (p1, k1) 3 times, p1.

Cont as now set, working as given for Left Front reversing Place Pocket shapings to *** and making buttonholes to correspond with markers on left front as follows:

Buttonhole row 1: RS. Rib 3, cast off 1 st, patt to end.

Buttonhole row 2: In patt, casting on 1 st over st cast off on previous row.

SHAPE NECK AND COLLAR

Row 1: Rib 7, M1, patt 3tog, patt to end.

Row 2: Patt to last 8 sts, rib to end.

Row 3: Rib 8, M1, patt to end.

Row 4: Patt to last 9 sts, rib to end.

Cont as now set, working as given for Left Front, reversing shapings.

SLEEVES (make 2)

With 12 mm needles cast on 19 (19:23:23:23) sts.

Cont in patt as given for Back, at the same time inc 1 st at each end of the 5th and 1 (1:6:6:1) foll 4th (4th:6th:6th:4th) rows [23 (23:37:37:27) sts], then on the 6 (6:0:0:6) foll 6th rows. [35 (35:37:37:39) sts.]

Cont straight until Sleeve measures 18 in. (46 cm) from beg, ending with a WS row.

SHAPE SLEEVE TOP

Cast off 2 (2:3:3:4) sts at beg of the next 2 rows [31 sts], then dec 1 st at each end of the next and 3 (3:5:5:6) foll alt rows [23 (23:19:19:17) sts], then on the next 3 (3:1:1:0) rows. Cast off rem 17 sts.

FINISHING

Join shoulders. Sew sleeve tops into armholes then join side and sleeve seams.

Sew pocket linings in position. Sew ends of collar together and sew in position at back of neck. Sew on buttons.

hooded cardigan with embroidery

An easy-to-wear, cozy ribbed and cabled cardigan with hood. Cross stitches have been worked in a complementary color to add a fun detail to the sweater.

By Hilary Mackin, from her book *Simple Stylish Knits*

BEGINNER

MEASUREMENTS

To fit bust

in.	32–34	36–38	40–42
cm	81–86	91–97	102–107

Actual width

in.	36½	41¼	44¼
cm	92.5	105	112.5

Actual length (from shoulder)

28 in. (71 cm)

Actual sleeve seam

in.	17¼	18	18½
cm	44	46	47

➤ In the instructions figures are given for the smallest size first; larger sizes follow in brackets. Where only one set of figures is given, this applies to all sizes.

MATERIALS

- 11 (12:13) × 50 g balls of Rowan Cork 047
- 1 × 50 g ball of Rowan Handknit DK Cotton for embroidery in 313
- Pair each of 7 mm and 8 mm needles
- Cable needle
- Stitch holders
- 28 in. (71 cm) open-ended zip

GAUGE

16 sts and 19 rows to 4 in. (10 cm) measured over pattern using 8 mm needles.

ABBREVIATIONS

C6 - slip 3 sts onto a cable needle and hold at front, k3 then k3 from cable needle.

See also page 7.

CARDIGAN

BACK

With 7 mm needles cast on 74 (84:90) sts.

1st and 3rd sizes

Row 1: RS. K1, p1, *k6, p2; rep from * to last 8 sts, k6, p1, k1.

Row 2: K2, *p6, k2; rep from * to end.

2nd size

Row 1: RS. K5, *p2, k6; rep from * to last 7 sts, p2, k5.

Row 2: K1, p4, *k2, p6; rep from * to last 7 sts, k2, p4, k1.

All sizes

Work a further 10 rows as now set.

Change to 8 mm needles. Cont in patt as follows:

1st size

Row 13: K1, p1, *C6, p2, k6, p2; rep from * to last 8 sts, C6, p1, k1.

Row 14: K2, *p6, k2; rep from * to end.

2nd size

Row 13: K5, *p2, C6, p2, k6; rep from * to last 15 sts, p2, C6, p2, k5.

Row 14: K1, p4, *k2, p6; rep from * to last 7 sts, k2, p4, k1.

3rd size

Row 13: K1, p1, *k6, p2, C6, p2; rep from * to last 8 sts, k6, p1, k1.

Row 14: K2, *p6, k2; rep from * to end.

All sizes

Rows 15, 17, 19, 21, and 23: As row 1.

Rows 16, 18, 20, 22, and 24: As row 2.

Rep rows 13 to 24 throughout. Cont in patt until work measures 19 (18:17¼) in. (48 [46:44] cm) from beg, ending with a WS row.

SHAPE RAGLANS

Cast off 5 (6:7) sts at beg of the next 2 rows. [64 (72:76) sts.]

Next row: K2, k2tog, patt to the last 4 sts, k2tog-tbl, k2.

Next row: K1, p2, patt to last 3 sts, p2, k1.

Rep the last 2 rows 20 (22:24) times more, leave rem 22 (26:26) sts on a st holder.

Some knitting skill is needed to create the cable pattern and cross stitch embroidery.

LEFT FRONT

With 7 mm needles cast on 40 (45:48) sts.

1st and 3rd sizes

Row 1: RS. K1, p1, *k6, p2; rep from * to last 6 sts, (k1, p1) twice, k2.

Row 2: (K1, p1) 3 times, k2, *p6, k2; rep from * to end.

2nd size

Row 1: RS. K5, p2; *k6, p2; rep from * to last 6 sts, (k1, p1) twice, k2.

Row 2: (K1, p1) 3 times, k2, *p6, k2; rep from * to last 5 sts, p4, k1.

All sizes

Work a further 10 rows as now set. **

Change to 8 mm needles. Cont in patt as follows:

1st size

Row 13: K1, p1, *C6, p2, k6, p2; rep from * to last 6 sts, (k1, p1) twice, k2.

Row 14: (K1, p1) 3 times, k2, *p6, k2; rep from * to end.

2nd size

Row 13: K5, p2, *C6, p2, k6, p2; rep from * to last 6 sts, (k1, p1) twice, k2.

Row 14: (K1, p1) 3 times, k2, *p6, k2; rep from * to last 5 sts, p4, k1.

Cross Stitch. This can be worked individually (as here) or in blocks. Work a row of diagonal stitches from left to right and complete the crosses by working diagonal stitches back from right to left. Choose a nice contrasting color.

3rd size

Row 13: K1, p1, *k6, p2, C6, p2; rep from * to last 14 sts, k6, p2, (k1, p1) twice, k2.

Row 14: (K1, p1) 3 times, k2, *p6, k2; rep from * to end.

All sizes

Rows 15 to 24: As Back.

Cont in patt as given for Back until work measures same as Back to beg of raglan shaping, ending with a WS row (RS on right front).

SHAPE RAGLAN

Cast off 5 (6:7) sts at beg of the next row. [35 (39:41) sts]. Work 1 row. (Omit this row on Right Front.)

Next row: K2, k2tog, patt to end.

Next row: Patt to last 3 sts, p2, k1.

Rep these 2 rows, 20 (22:24) times more. [14 (16:16) sts.] Leave sts on a st holder.

RIGHT FRONT

Work as given for Left Front to **.

Change to 8 mm needles. Cont in patt as follows:

1st size

Row 13: K2, (p1, k1) twice, *p2, k6, p2, C6; rep from * to last 2 sts, p1, k1.

2nd size

Row 13: K2, (p1, k1) twice, p2, *k6, p2, C6, p2; rep from * to last 5 sts, k5.

3rd size

Row 13: K2, (p1, k1) twice, p2; *k6, p2, C6, p2; rep from * to last 8 sts, k6, p1, k1.

Cont as now set. Complete as given for Left Front, reversing shapings, ending with a WS row. Leave sts on a st holder.

SLEEVES (make 2)

With 7 mm needles cast on 34 (38:42) sts.

Row 1: RS. P0 (0:2), k4 (6:6), *p2, k6; rep from * to last 6 (8:10) sts, p2, k4 (6:6), p0 (0:2).

Row 2: K0 (0, 2), p4 (6:6), k2, *p6, k2; rep from * to last 4 (6:8) sts, p4 (6:6), k0 (0:2).

Work a further 10 rows as now set.

Change to 8 mm needles. **

Row 13: P0 (0 2), k4 (6:6), p2, C6, p2, k6, p2, C6, p2, k4 (6:6), p0 (0:2).

Rep rows 13 to 24 as given for Back, at the same time inc 1 st at each end of the foll 4th and 0 (0:1) foll 4th rows [36 (40:46) sts], then on the 9 (10:10) foll 6th rows [54 (60:66) sts], working patt into inc sts.

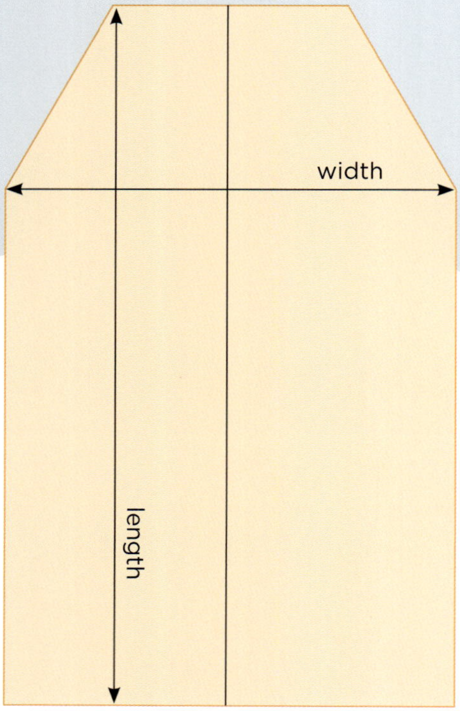

Inserting the zipper requires neat finishing.

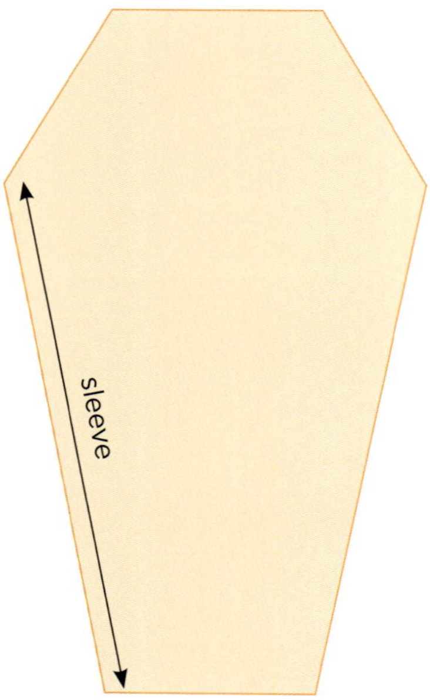

Cont straight until sleeve measures 17¼ (18:18½) in. (44 [46:47] cm) from beg, ending with a WS row.

SHAPE RAGLANS

Cast off 5 (6:7) sts at beg of the next 2 rows. [44 (48:52) sts.]

Row 1: K2, k2tog, patt to last 4 sts, k2tog-tbl, k2.

Rows 2 and 4: K1, p2, patt to last 3 sts, p2, k1.

Row 3: K3, patt to last 3 sts, k3.

Rep the last 4 rows, 4 times more [34 (38:42) sts], then dec 1 st at each end of the next and 10 (12:14) foll alt rows. [12 sts.]

Work 1 row. Leave sts on a st holder.

HOOD

Join raglans.

With right side facing and 8 mm needles, rib 6, k8 (10:10) sts from right front st holder, knit across 12 sts from top of right sleeve, work across 22 (26:26) sts from back neck as follows:

K6 (7:7), M1, (k5 (6:6), M1) twice, k6 (7:7), knit across 12 sts from top of left sleeve, then 8 (10:10) sts from left front, rib rem 6 sts as set. [77 (85:85) sts.]

Cont in st st beg with a purl row, keeping the 6 rib sts at each end on every row, until hood measures 13¾ in. (35 cm) from beg, ending with a WS row. Cast off.

FINISHING

Join hood seam. Join side and sleeve seams.

Sew in zip. Make a tassel using 6 strands of yarn approximately 10 in. (25 cm) long (see Making Tassels, page 10). Fold in half, wind yarn ½ in. (1.5 cm) down from folded end and secure, thread yarn through loop formed and attach to point on back hood.

Work embroidered cross stitches on each rib between cables.

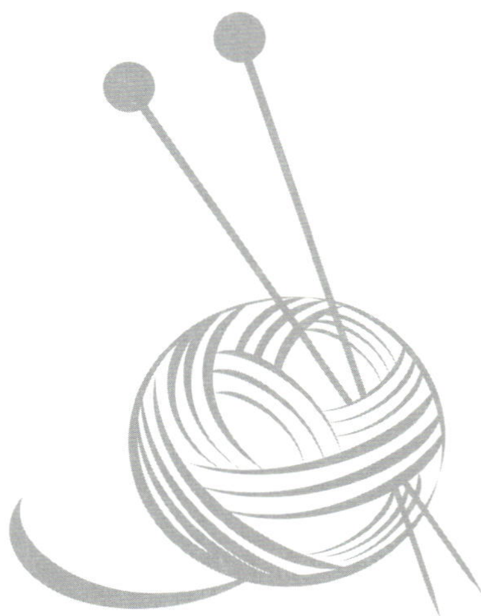

turtle neck sweater

Keep nice and cozy in this figure-hugging ribbed sweater with a deep turnover collar and three-quarter length sleeves. It will look equally good over a skirt or jeans! Worked in a wide rib pattern that is very simple to follow, even the less experienced knitter will be able to complete this project.

By Val Pierce, from her book *Love Knitting*

INTERMEDIATE

MEASUREMENTS

Bust size: 34/36 in. (86/92 cm)
Length from back neck to hem: 25 in. (64 cm)
Sleeve length: 13 in. (33 cm)

MATERIALS

- 10 x 50 g balls of Patons Merino wool DK (shade 00032)
- Pair of 3¾ mm (US 5/UK 9) needles
- Pair of 4 mm (US 6/UK 8) needles
- Stitch holders

GAUGE

22 sts x 30 rows over stocking stitch = 4 in. (10 cm) using 4 mm (UK 8/US 6) needles

ABBREVIATIONS

See page 7.

When measuring the length of the pieces, pull out to the correct width on a flat surface as rib patterns tend to draw the work in.

BACK

Using 3¾ mm (US 5/UK 9) needles, cast on 103 sts.

Now commence pattern as follows:

Row 1 (RS): K2, *p3, k3. Rep from * to last 5 sts, p3, k2.

Row 2: P2, *k3, p3. Rep from * to last 5 sts, k3, p2.

Repeat the last 2 rows 7 times more.

Change to 4 mm (US 6/ UK 8) needles and continue in rib as set until work measures 18 in. (45 cm), ending on a WS row (pull out piece to size before measuring the length).

SHAPE ARMHOLES

Cast off 3 sts in pattern at the beginning of the next 2 rows.

Decrease 1 st at each end of next 7 rows, then every alternate row until 75 sts remain. ****

Work straight until armhole measures 7 in. (18 cm), ending with a WS row.

SHAPE SHOULDERS

Cast off 5 sts in pattern at the beginning of the next 6 rows, then 3 sts at the beginning of the following 2 rows. Slip the remaining 39 sts onto a holder for the neckband.

FRONT

Work as back until **** is reached.

Work straight until armhole measures 5 in. (13 cm), ending with a WS row.

SHAPE NECK

Row 1: Work 27 sts and turn, complete this side first.

Decrease 1 st at neck edge of next 5 rows, then every alternate row until 18 sts remain. Work straight until armhole measures the same as back, ending at side edge.

SHAPE SHOULDERS

Cast off 5 sts at beginning of next and every alternate row until 3 sts remain. Work 1 row and cast off. Slip center 21 sts onto a holder for neckband. Rejoin yarn to neck edge of remaining stitches and work to end. Complete as given for first side, reversing shapings.

SLEEVES

Using 4 mm (US 6/ UK 8) needles, cast on 61 sts.

Proceed in pattern as set on back for 8 rows.

Taking extra stitches into pattern, increase 1 st each end of next and every following 10th row until there are 69 sts on the needle. Proceed without further shaping until sleeve measures 13 in. (33 cm) ending with a WS row.

SHAPE SLEEVE TOP

Cast off 3 sts at the beginning of the next 2 rows. Dec 1 st at each end of the next and following alternate rows until 35 sts remain. Dec 1 st at each end of the next 4 rows. Now cast off 4 sts at the beginning of the next 2 rows (19 sts). Cast off remaining stitches.

Make other sleeve to match.

FINISHING AND COLLAR

Join left shoulder seam. With RS facing and using 3¾ mm (US 5/UK 9) needles, work across sts on holder at back neck, pick up and knit 24 sts down left neck slope, work across sts on front neck holder, pick up and knit 24 sts up right front neck slope. (108 sts.) Keeping continuity of rib pattern correct, continue until work measures 4 in. (10 cm). Now change to 4 mm (US 6/UK 8) needles and work until collar measures 8 in. (20 cm). Cast off loosely in rib pattern. Join right shoulder seam and collar seam. Join side and sleeve seams. Insert sleeves.

sweater with frilled hem and cuffs

This lovely sweater is knitted using a textured yarn and has a panel of knit/purl diagonal stitches on the front and back. The bell edging detail on the cuffs and lower hem make this a pretty, feminine sweater.

By Hilary Mackin, from her book *Simple Stylish Knits*

BEGINNER

MEASUREMENTS

To fit bust

in.	32	34	36	38	40
cm	81	86	91	97	102

Actual width

in.	34¾	36¾	38½	40½	42½
cm	88	93	98	103	108

Actual length

in.	21	21	21¼	21¾	22
cm	53	53	54	55	56

Actual sleeve seam

in.	17½	18½	18½	18½	18½
cm	44	47	47	47	47

➤ In the instructions figures are given for the smallest size first; larger sizes follow in brackets. Where only one set of figures is given, this applies to all sizes.

MATERIALS

- 9 (9:10:10:11) x 50 g hanks of Rowan Summer Tweed in 508
- Pair of 5 mm needles
- Stitch holders

GAUGE

16 sts and 23 rows to 4 in. (10 cm) measured over stocking stitch using 5 mm needles.

ABBREVIATIONS

See page 7.

SWEATER

BACK AND FRONT (alike)

With 5 mm needles cast on 207 (219:231:243:255) sts and work bell edge patt as follows:

Rows 1 and 3: RS. P3, *k9, p3; rep from * to end.

Rows 2 and 4: K3, *p9, k3; rep from * to end.

Row 5: P3, *yb, sl 1, k1, psso, k5, k2tog, p3; rep from * to end.

Rows 6 and 8: K3, *p7, k3; rep from * to end.

Row 7: P3, *k7, p3; rep from * to end.

Row 9: P3, *yb, sl 1, k1, psso, k3, k2tog, p3; rep from * to end.

Rows 10 and 12: K3, *p5, k3; rep from * to end.

Row 11: P3, *k5, p3; rep from * to end.

Row 13: P3, *yb, sl 1, k1, psso, k1, k2tog, p3; rep from * to end.

Rows 14 and 16: K3, *p3, k3; rep from * to end.

Row 15: P3, *k3, p3; rep from * to end.

Row 17: P3, *yb, sl 1, k2tog, psso, p3; rep from * to end.

Row 18: K3, *p1, k3; rep from * to end.

These 18 rows form the bell edge. [71 (75:79:83:87) sts.]

Cont as follows:

Row 1: K19 (21:23:25:27), p1, k1b, (p2, k2) 7 times, p1, k1b, p1, k19 (21:23:25:27).

Row 2: P19 (21:23:25:27), k1, p1, k2, (p2, k2) 6 times, p2, k1, p1, k1, p19 (21:23:25:27).

Row 3: K19 (21:23:25:27), p1, k1b, (k2, p2) 7 times, k1, k1b, p1, k19 (21:23:25:27).

Row 4: P19 (21:23:25:27), k1, p3, (k2, p2) 7 times, k1, p19 (21:23:25:27).

These 4 rows form the patt. Cont in patt until work measures 13½ in. (34 cm) from beg, ending with a WS row.

SHAPE ARMHOLES

Cast off 3 (3:4:4:5) sts at beg of the next 2 rows [65 (69:71:75:77) sts], then dec 1 st at each end of the 5 (5:6:6:7) foll alt rows. [55 (59:59:63:63) sts.]

Cont straight in patt until armhole measures 6 (6:6¼:6½:7) in. (15 [15:16:17:18] cm) from beg of shaping, ending with a WS row.

Creating the frilled edges requires some skill.

Helpful Hint. When measuring your work, lay the pieces out on a flat surface and smooth out, without stretching. This will guarantee accurate measurements.

SHAPE NECK

K18 (19:19:20:20), turn and leave rem sts on a st holder, work on these sts for first side. Work 10 rows, dec 1 st at neck edge on every row. Work 1 row. Cast off rem 8 (9:9:10:10) sts.

With RS facing, slip the center 19 (21:21:23:23) sts on a st holder, rejoin yarn and patt to end. Complete this side to match first side, reversing shapings.

SLEEVES **(make 2)**

With 5 mm needles cast on 87 (87:99:99:111) sts and work the 18 rows of bell edge as given for Back. [31 (31:35:35:39) sts.]

Cont in st st beg with a knit row, at the same time inc 1 st at each end of the 3rd and 3 foll 4th rows [39 (39:43:43:47) sts], then on the 8 (9:9:9:9) foll 8th rows. [55 (57:61:61:65) sts.] Cont straight until sleeve measures 17½ (18½:18½:18½:18½) in. (44 [47:47:47:47] cm) from beg, ending with a WS row.

SHAPE SLEEVE TOP

Cast off 3 (3:4:4:5) sts at beg of the next 2 rows [49 (51:53:53:55) sts], then dec 1 st at each end of the next and 8 (7:8:8:11) foll alt rows [31 (35:35:35:31) sts], then on the next 9 (11:11:11:9) rows. Cast off rem 13 sts.

NECKBAND

Join left shoulder.

With 5 mm needles, knit up 9 sts down right back neck, knit across 19 (21:21:23:23) sts from st holder, knit up 9 sts up left back neck, 9 sts down left front neck, knit across 19 (21:21:23:23) sts from st holder, knit up 9 sts up right front neck. [74 (78:78:82:82) sts.] Knit 1 row. Cast off.

FINISHING

Join right shoulder.

Sew sleeve tops into armholes then join side and sleeve seams.

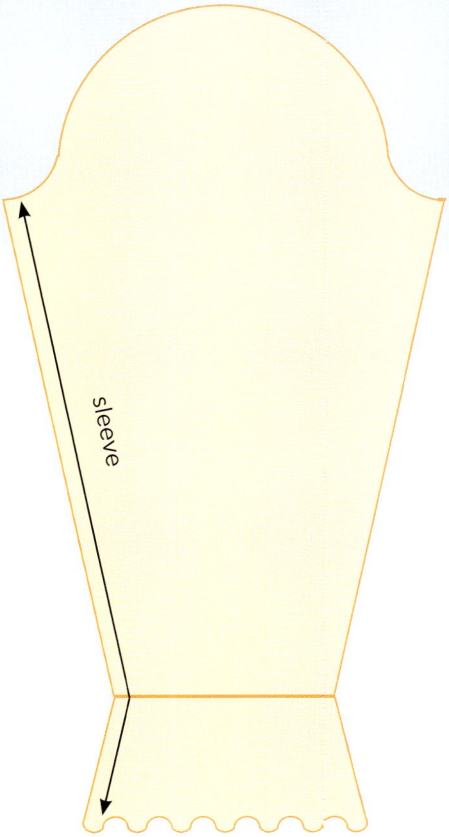
sleeve

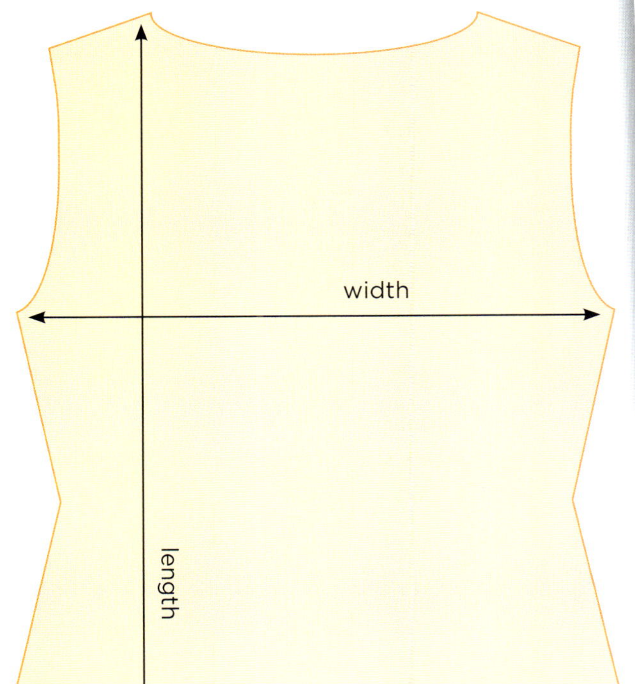
width
length

sweater with lace collar and cuffs

Worked in a sparkly lurex yarn, this slim-fitting sweater would look good at any special occasion teamed with trousers or skirt. It is knitted in stocking stitch with a lace garter stitch border, which is made separately and sewn on afterward.

By Hilary Mackin, from her book *Simple Stylish Knits*

BEGINNER

MEASUREMENTS

To fit bust

in.	32	34	36	38	40
cm	81	91	97	102	107

Actual width

in.	29½	32	33½	36	37¾
cm	75	81	85	91	96

Actual length

in.	18	18½	19	19	19¼
cm	46	47	48	48	49

Actual sleeve seam (with cuff lace edging)

in.	18	19¼	19¼	19¼	19¼
cm	46	49	49	49	49

➤ In the instructions figures are given for the smallest size first; larger sizes follow in brackets. Where only one set of figures is given, this applies to all sizes.

MATERIALS

- 14 (15:16:17:18) x 25 g balls of Rowan Lurex in Antique White Gold
- Pair each of 2¾ mm, 3¼ mm and 4 mm needles
- Stitch holder

GAUGE

29 sts and 41 rows to 4 in. (10 cm) measured over stocking stitch using 3¼ mm needles.

ABBREVIATIONS

See page 7.

Allow a little more time to complete this project as metallic yarn does take longer to work with.

SWEATER

BACK AND FRONT (alike)

With 2¾ mm needles cast on 110 (118:124:132:140) sts and knit 10 rows.

Change to 3¼ mm needles. Cont in st st beg with a knit row, shaping sides by dec 1 st at each end of the 5th and 5 foll 6th rows [98 (106:112:120:128) sts], then inc 1 st at each end of the 6 foll 12th rows. [110 (118:124:132:140) sts.]

Cont straight until work measures 13½ in. (34 cm) from beg, ending with a WS row.

SHAPE RAGLANS

Cast off 6 (6:7:7:8) sts at beg of the next 2 rows [98 (106:110:118:124) sts], then dec 1 st at each end of the next and 0 (2:4:8:12) foll alt rows [96 (100:100:100:98) sts], then on the 10 (10:10:8:7) foll 4th rows. [76 (80:80:84:84) sts.] Work 1 row, ending with a WS row.

SHAPE FRONT NECK

Knit 10, turn and leave rem 66 (70:70:74:74) sts on a st holder. Work on these sts for first side.

Cast off 4 sts at neck edge on next row. Dec 1 st at each end of the next row, then 1 st at neck edge on the next 3 rows. Fasten off last st.

The lace pattern on the collar and cuffs requires some knitting skill.

Helpful Hints

➤ Sew the collar to the neck edge using a firm back stitch to avoid the neckline stretching too much.

➤ When buying lurex or glittery metallic yarns, make sure they have a polyester base as some materials will tarnish or lose their shine over time.

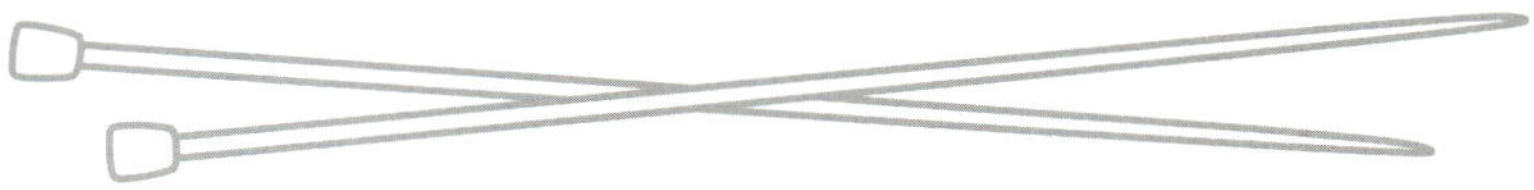

With RS facing, rejoin yarn to center sts. Cast off 56 (60:60:64:64) sts and knit to end. [10 sts.] Complete this side to match first side, reversing shapings.

SLEEVES (make 2)

With 3¼ mm needles cast on 58 (58:64:64:66) sts. Cont in st st beg with a knit row, shaping sides by inc 1 st at each end of the 3rd and 2 (7:7:7:13) foll 4th rows, then on the 17 (15:15:15:11) foll 6th rows. [98 (104:110:110:116) sts.] Cont straight until Sleeve measures 33 (36:36:36:36) cm (13 (14:14:14:14) in) from beg, ending with a WS row.

SHAPE RAGLAN

Cast off 6 (6:7:7:8) sts at beg of the next 2 rows. [86 (92:96:96:100) sts.] Dec 1 st at each end of the next and 20 (24:26:26:28) foll alt rows [44 (42:42:42:42) sts], then on the 1 (0:0:0:0) foll 4th row. [42 sts.] Work 3 rows. Cast off.

FINISHING

Join 3 raglans leaving right back seam open.

NECKBAND

With RS facing and 2¾ mm needles, knit up 56 (60:60:64:64) sts from back, 37 sts from top of left sleeve, 56 (60:60:64:64) sts from front, 37 sts from top of right sleeve. [186 (194:194:202:202) sts.]

Knit 9 rows. Cast off. Join remaining raglan and neckband.

Join side and sleeve seams.

LACE FRILL NECKBAND

With 4 mm needles, cast on 25 sts and knit 1 row.

Row 1: Sl 1, k6, (yo, k2tog) 8 times, yo, k2.

Rows 2, 4, 6, 8, and 10: Knit.

Row 3: Sl 1, k9, (yo, k2tog) 7 times, yo, k2.

Row 5: Sl 1, k12, (yo, k2tog) 6 times, yo, k2.

Row 7: Sl 1, k15, (yo, k2tog) 5 times, yo, k2.

Row 9: Sl 1, k18, (yo, k2tog) 4 times, yo, k2.

Row 11: Sl 1, k29.

Row 12: Cast off 5 sts, k to end. [25 sts.]

These 12 rows form the lace edge patt.

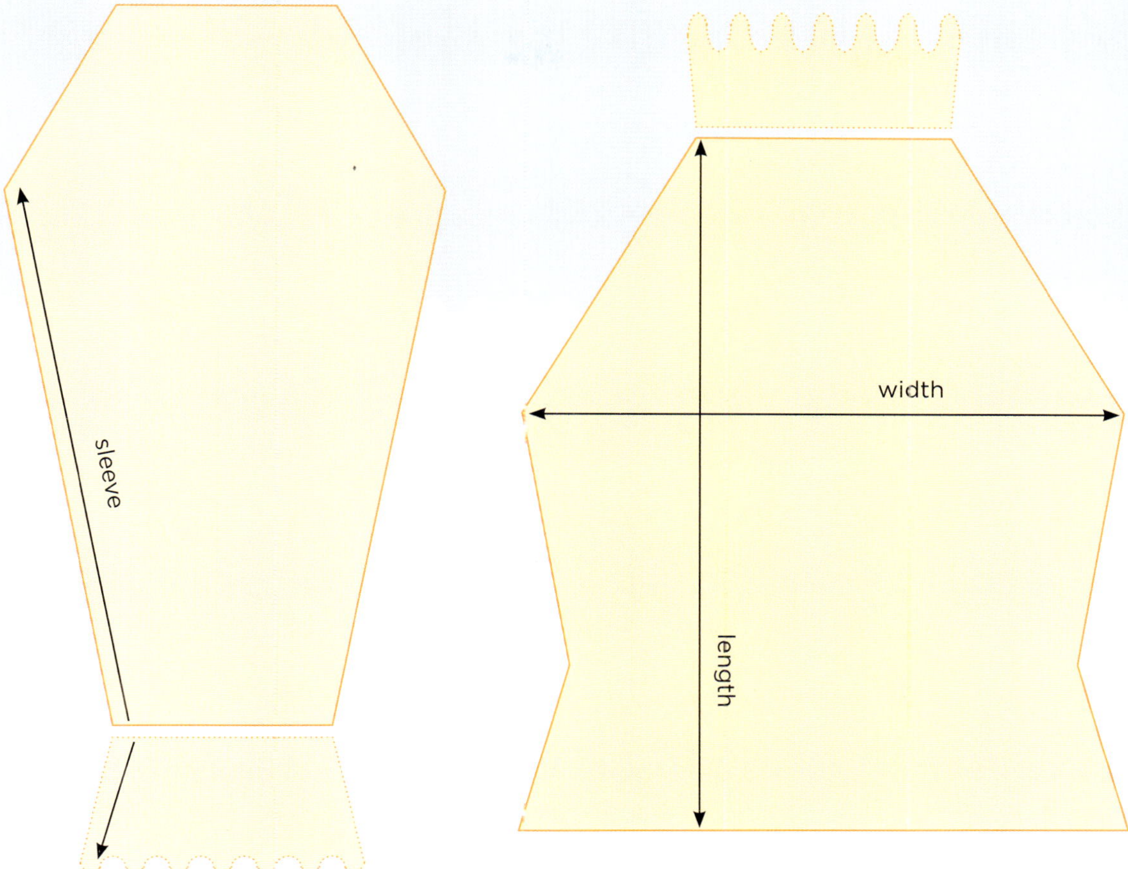

Cont in patt until piece fits around neck edge. Do not stretch the fabric when measuring. Cast off.

Join cast-on and cast-off edges, then with RS of frill to WS body and seam to right back raglan seam, sew around neck edge firmly using a back stitch.

LACE FRILL CUFFS (make 2)

With 4 mm needles, cast on 25 sts and knit 1 row.

Work the 12 rows of patt as given for neckband until piece fits around cuff edge. Cast off. Join cast-on and cast-off edge, then with seam to sleeve seam, sew around cuffs edge firmly using a back stitch.

lacy wrist warmers

The soft cashmere and pure wool are combined with two fairly simple lacy stitches to create these elegant wrist warmers. Wear them to go with your favorite outfit or use them for extra warmth on a cool morning.

By Val Pierce, from her book *Love Knitting*

INTERMEDIATE

MEASUREMENTS

Length: 8½ in. (21 cm) (to fit an average lady's hand), but the fabric is quite stretchy. If you require a longer finished measurement, just add extra rows before the finishing garter stitch edging, bearing in mind that you may need extra yarn.

MATERIALS

- 2 x 50 g balls of Rowan Cashsoft 4-ply (shade 422 Black)
- Pair of 3¾ mm (US 5/UK 9) needles
- Pair of 4 mm (US 6/UK 8) needles

GAUGE

Not critical

ABBREVIATIONS

skpso - sl1, k1. Pass slipped stitch over the knitted one.
See also page 7.

WRIST WARMERS

SCALLOPED EDGE

Using 3¾ mm (US 5/UK 9) needles, cast on 113 sts.

Now commence pattern as follows:

Row 1: Purl.

Row 2 (RS): K2, *k1, slip this st back onto left-hand needle, lift the next 8 sts on left-hand needle over this st and off the needle, yo twice, knit the first st again, k2. Rep from *.

Row 3: K1, *p2tog, (k1, k1tbl) into yo loops, p1. Rep from * to last st, k1. (42 sts remain.)

Now commence lacy pattern as follows:

Row 1 (RS): K1, *k2tog, yo, k1, yo, skpso, repeat from * to last st, k1.

Row 2: Purl.

These two rows form the pattern and are repeated throughout.

When work measures 8½ in. (21 cm) ending on a purl row, change to 3¾ mm (UK 9/US 5) needles and work 4 rows in quite firm garter stitch, then cast off.

Make other wrist warmer to match.

FINISHING

Note: Side seams will run up the inside of the wrists.

Work in all ends neatly. Sew side seams, remembering to leave an opening for the thumb in the relevant place. Catch together garter stitch rows at top of piece.

snuggle alpaca shawl

Snuggle into this luxurious shawl, created with the softest baby alpaca yarn. The shawl is made in simple garter stitch, with the addition of a lacy border, which is knitted separately and sewn on. The lace is a simple 8-row pattern repeat, but if you can't manage the lace, then leave it out; it will look just as pretty!

By Val Pierce, from her book *Love Knitting*

INTERMEDIATE

MEASUREMENTS

Width: 56 in. (142 cm)

Depth: 30 in. (76 cm)

Lace edging will add an extra 2 in. (5 cm) on width and depth

MATERIALS

- 7 x 50 g balls of RY Baby Alpaca DK (shade 205 Jacob)
- Pair of 5 mm (US 8/UK 6) needles
- Circular needle size 5 mm (US 8/UK 6)
- Blunt-ended sewing needle

GAUGE

20 sts over garter stitch = 4 in. (10 cm) using 5 mm (US 8/UK 6) needles

ABBREVIATIONS

See page 7.

SHAWL

Using 5 mm (US 8/UK 6) needles, cast on 1 st.

Now commence pattern as follows:

Next row: Knit twice into stitch.

Next row: K1, knit twice into next stitch.

Next row: K1, inc in next st, k1.

Next row: K1, inc in next st, knit to end.

Continue to inc 1 st at the beginning of every row as set until you have 210 sts on the needle. Cast off. When stitches become too many for ordinary needles, change to the circular needle and work back and forth.

LACE EDGING

Using 5 mm (US 8/UK 6) needles, cast on 12 sts.

Now commence pattern as follows:

Row 1: K3, yfwd, k5, yfwd, k2tog, yfwd, k2.

Row 2: K2, p12.

Row 3: K4, sl1, k2tog, psso, k2, (yfwd, k2tog) twice, k1.

Row 4: K2, p10.

Row 5: K3, sl1, k1, psso, k2, (yfwd, k2tog) twice, k1.

Row 6: K2, p9.

Row 7: K2, sl1, k1, psso, k2, (yfwd, k2tog) twice, k1.

Row 8: K2, p8.

Row 9: K1, sl1, k1, psso, k2, (yfwd, k2tog) twice, k1.

Row 10: K2, p7.

Row 11: Sl1, k1, psso, k2, yfwd, k1, yfwd, k2tog, yfwd, k2.

Row 12: K2, p8.

Row 13: (K3, yfwd) twice, k2tog, yfwd, k2.

Row 14: K2, p10.

These 14 rows form the pattern and are repeated throughout. Continue in pattern until lace strip is long enough to go around the two side edges of the shawl, ending on a Row 14. Cast off.

FINISHING

Work in all ends neatly. Pin edging in place around the two side edges, gather slightly to fit around the point of the shawl. Sew in place using a flat seam.

beaded "denim" belt

A simple two-row pattern and just two balls of yarn are all that are needed to make this pretty beaded belt. The fringe is very easy to work and adds a little sparkle to the finished piece. Use my color choice or choose a shade of yarn and matching beads to complement your favorite outfit.

By Val Pierce, from her book *Love Knitting*

BEGINNER

MEASUREMENTS

Width: 2 in. (5 cm)

Length: 52 in. (132 cm)

MATERIALS

- 2 x 50 g balls of Patons Merino Wool DK Denim (shade 00051)
- Pair of 4 mm (UK 8/US 6) needles
- 1 x 5 mm (UK 6/US 8) needle
- 30 x 10 mm (¼ in.) crystal beads

GAUGE

Not critical

ABBREVIATIONS

See page 7.

BELT

Using 4 mm (UK 8/US 6) needles, cast on 16 sts.

Now commence pattern as follows:

Row 1: K3, p1, *k2, p1* 3 times. K3.

Row 2: K1, *yfwd, k2 (pass the yfwd over the last 2 knitted stitches), k1* 5 times.

These two rows form the pattern and are repeated throughout.

Continue as set until belt measures 52 in. (132 cm), or the desired length. Cast off.

BEADED FRINGES

Make 10 pieces, 5 for each end of the belt.

Using 4 mm (UK 8/US 6) needles, cast on 36 sts.

Change to the 5 mm (UK 6/US 8) needle and cast off. The fringe will automatically curl as you cast off.

FINISHING

Stitch in any ends neatly. Sew 3 beads, evenly spaced onto each fringe, then sew the fringe to the belt ends.

toasty slippers

An ideal project for the beginner, these soft and cozy slippers are knitted in simple garter stitch using big needles. You can make them in just a weekend! The flower embellishments are a little more time-consuming to make but they are worth the extra effort when they are completed.

By Val Pierce, from her book *Love Knitting*

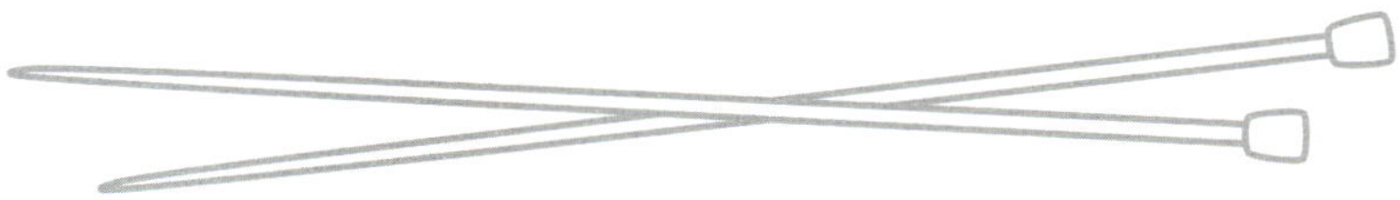

BEGINNER

MEASUREMENTS

One size (to fit an average lady's foot)

MATERIALS

- 3 x 50 g balls of Twilleys Freedom Wool (shade 420 Olive)
- Oddments of contrasting yarn in DK weight for flowers
- Pair of 6 mm (US 10/UK 4) needles
- Pair of 4 mm (US 6/UK 8) needles
- 2 decorative buttons

GAUGE

14 sts x 20 rows over stocking stitch = 4 in. (10 cm) using 6 mm (US 10/UK 4) needles

ABBREVIATIONS

See page 7.

LEFT SLIPPER

With 6 mm (UK 4/US 10) needles, cast on 48 sts, knit 1 row.

Next row: (K2, m1, k1) twice, knit to last 6 sts, (k1, m1, k2) twice. (52 sts.)

Next row: Knit.

Repeat the last 2 rows once more. (56 sts.)

Next row: K25, (k1, m1) 6 times, knit to end. (62 sts.)

Knit 12 rows.

SHAPE FOOT

Next row: K19, (k2tog) 12 times, knit to end. (50 sts.)

Next row: K33, turn.

Next row: (K2tog) 8 times, k1, turn.

Next row: K10, turn.

Next row: (K2tog) 5 times, knit to end.

Knit 1 row, cast off fairly loosely knit-wise.

STRAP

Count 9 sts in from back seam, pick up and knit 4 sts from cast-off edge.

Working on these 4 sts, continue in garter stitch for 22 rows.

Next row: K2, yrn twice, k2.

Next row: K2, drop extra loop of yrn, knit it and the next st together, k1.

Next row: (K2tog) twice.

Next row: K2tog and fasten off.

RIGHT SLIPPER

Work as left slipper but remember to pick up and knit the stitches for the strap on the opposite side of the foot.

FLOWER (make 2)

Using 4 mm (UK 8/US 6) needles and DK weight yarn, cast on 57 sts.

Row 1: Purl.

Row 2: K2, *k1, slip this st back onto left-hand needle, lift the next 8 sts on left-hand needle over this st and off the needle, yo twice, knit the first st again, k2. Rep from *.

Row 3: K1, *p2tog, (k1, k1tbl) into loops made on previous row, p1. Repeat from * to last st, k1. Do not cast off, run yarn through stitches on needle and draw up into a circle to form flower. Sew edge together.

FINISHING

Work in all ends neatly. Sew the foot seam of the slipper. Attach a button to correspond with the buttonhole in the strap. Stitch a flower to the center front of each slipper.

two-color cape

This easy-to-wear, cozy cape is knitted in two different colors and yarns which complement each other. Garter stitch ridges add extra texture.

By Hilary Mackin, from her book *Simple Stylish Knits*

BEGINNER

MEASUREMENTS

To fit bust

in.	32–36	38–42
cm	81–91	97–107

Actual length (excluding fringing)

in.	22¾	23¾
cm	58	60

Actual width round lower edge

in.	71	78
cm	180	198

➤ In the instructions figures are given for the smallest size first; larger size follows in brackets. Where only one set of figures is given this applies to both sizes.

MATERIALS

- 3 (4) x 100 g balls of Rowan Plaid in Red 156 (A)
- 4 (5) x 100 g balls of Rowan Chunky Print in Black 079 (B)
- Pair each of 6 mm and 8 mm needles
- Stitch holders
- 2 buttons (1 large, 1 small)

GAUGE

11½ sts and 15½ rows to 4 in. (10 cm) measured over stocking stitch using 8 mm needles.

ABBREVIATIONS

See page 7.

CAPE

RIGHT SIDE **(back and front worked in one piece)**

With 6 mm needles and A, cast on 104 (114) sts. Knit 4 rows.

Change to 8 mm needles. Cont in patt as follows:

Work 8 rows in st st, beg with a knit row.

Row 13 (dec row): K25 (28), sl 1, k1, psso, k50 (54), k2tog, k25 (28). [102 (112) sts.]

St st 5 more rows. Knit 4 rows.

Row 23 (dec row): K25 (28), sl 1, k1, psso, k48 (52), k2tog, k25 (28). [100 (110) sts.]

Knit 1 row.

Work 8 rows in st st.

Row 33 (dec row): K25 (28), sl 1, k1, psso, k46 (50), k2tog, k25 (28). [98 (108) sts.]

St st 5 more rows.

Cont in this way, working patt - 6 rows in g st and 14 rows in st st throughout, at the same time dec in the same way as before on the next and foll 6th row. [94 (104) sts.]

Then dec on the 3 foll 4th rows, then on the 18 (20) foll alt rows. [52 (58) sts.]

Work 1 row.

Next row: K25 (28), sl 1, k1, psso, k25 (28). [51 (57) sts.]

Next row: Purl.

Next row: K4, *k2tog, k5(2); rep from * 6 (12) times, k2tog, k3. [44 sts.]

Next row: Purl and leave sts on a st holder.

LEFT SIDE **(back and front worked in one piece)**

With 6 mm needles and B, cast on 104 (114) sts. Knit 4 rows.

Change to 8 mm needles and cont as given for Right Side.

FINISHING

Join center back seam.

NECKBAND

With RS facing and using 6 mm needles and B, knit across 43 sts from right side, k2tog, knit rem 43 sts from left side. [87 sts.]

Knit 1 row. Cast off.

This is a really straightforward and simple pattern.

This pattern can be knitted in a short amount of time.

FRONT EDGES **(make 2)**

With RS facing and using 6 mm needles and B, knit up 78 sts along one front edge. Knit 1 row. Cast off.

Sew the large button 4¾ in. (12 cm) in from left front edge and the small button at the same distance on the wrong side on right front. Sew a loop on each top edge to correspond with buttons.

For each tassel cut 4 strands of yarn approximately 9¾ in. (25 cm) long, tie in fringing evenly along lower edge (see Making Tassels, page 10). Work fringing in A on front worked in B, and in B on front worked in A.

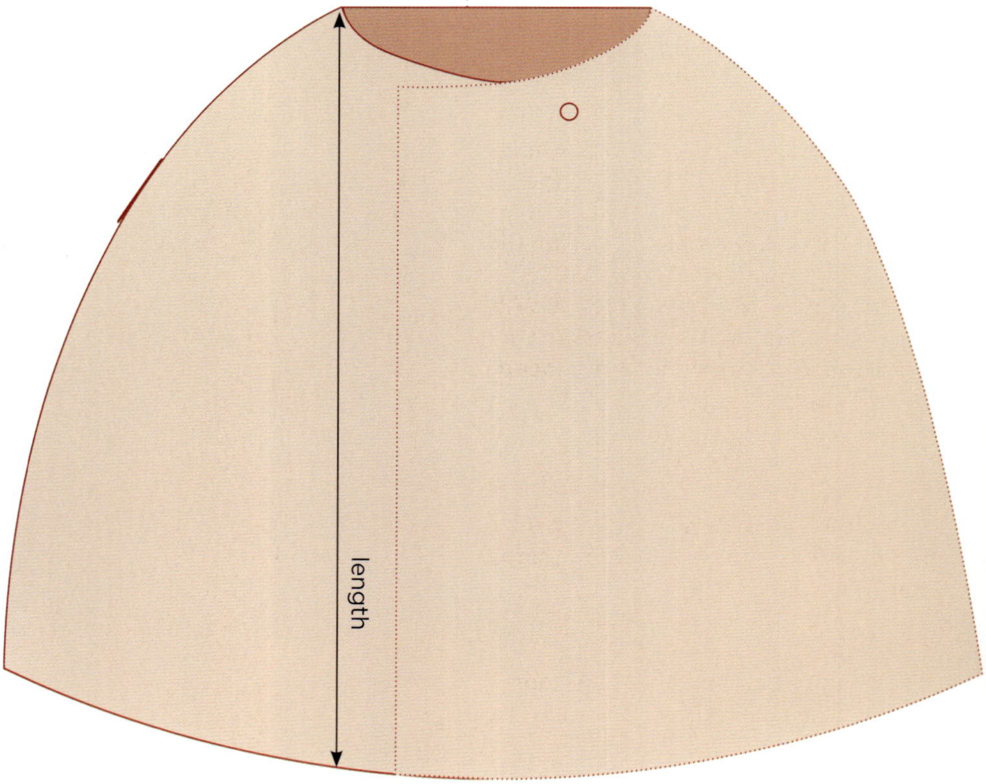

striped sleeveless top

Keep the chill off with this simple V-necked slipover. It is made using a chenille yarn to give it a luxurious look and is worked in stocking stitch with subtle striped color changes.

By Hilary Mackin, from her book *Simple Stylish Knits*

BEGINNER

MEASUREMENTS

To fit bust

in.	32	34	36	38	40
cm	81	86	91	97	102

Actual width

in.	32	34	36	38	40
cm	81	86	91	97	102

Actual length

in.	21½	22	22½	23	23¼
cm	55	56	57	58	59

➤ In the instructions figures are given for the smallest size first; larger sizes follow in brackets. Where only one set of figures is given, this applies to all sizes.

MATERIALS

- 2 (2:2:3:3) x 100 g balls of Rowan Chunky Cotton Chenille in Angel Tears 391 (A)
- 1 (1:1:2:2) x 100 g balls of Rowan Chunky Cotton Chenille in Flutter 389 (B)
- 1 (1:1:2:2) x 100 g balls of Rowan Chunky Cotton Chenille in Wraith 394 (C)
- Pair each of 4 mm and 5 mm needles
- Stitch holder
- Safety pin

GAUGE

15 sts and 26 rows to 4 in. (10 cm) measured over stocking stitch using 5 mm needles.

ABBREVIATIONS

2tog-tbl - work 2 stitches together through back of loops
See also page 7.

Keep the chill off with this simple V-necked slipover.

SLEEVELESS TOP

BACK

With 4 mm needles and A, cast on 61 (65:69:73:77) sts.

Row 1: RS *k1, p1; rep from * to last st, k1.

Row 2: *P1, k1; rep from * to last st, p1.

These 2 rows form the rib; work 4 more rows in rib.

Change to 5 mm needles. Cont in st st beg with a knit row and stripe patt, at the same time, shaping for sides as given below:

Stripe sequence: Work 6 rows in A, 4 rows in B, (2 rows in A, 2 rows in C), twice, 2 rows in A, 4 rows in B. These 24 rows form the patt and are repeated throughout. Cont in patt dec 1 st at both ends of the 5th and 4 foll 4th rows [51 (55:59:63:67) sts], then inc 1 st at both ends of the foll 12th and 4 foll 8th rows. [61 (65:69:73:77) sts.]

Cont straight in patt until work measures 13¾ in. (35 cm) from beg, ending with a WS row. **

SHAPE ARMHOLES

Cast off 4 (4:5:5:6) sts at beg of the next 2 rows [53 (57:59:63:65) sts], then dec 1 st at both ends of the next 4 rows [45 (49:51:55:57) sts], then on the 3 foll alt rows. [39 (43:45:49:51) sts.]

Cont straight in patt until armhole measures 8 (8¼:8½:9:9½) in. (20 [21:22:23:24] cm) from beg, ending with a WS row.

SHAPE SHOULDERS AND BACK OF NECK

Cast off 3 (4:4:5:5) sts at beg of the next row, knit until there are 8 (9:9:10:10) sts on RH needle after cast-off. Work on these sts for first side. Cast off 4 sts at neck edge on next row. Cast off rem 4 (5:5:6:6) sts.

With RS facing, slip the center 17 (17:19:19:21) sts on a st holder, rejoin yarn and knit to end. Complete as given for first side, reversing shapings.

FRONT

Work as given for Back to **.

SHAPE ARMHOLES AND DIVIDE FOR V-NECK

Cast off 4 (4:5:5:6) sts at beg of the next row, knit until there are 26 (28:29:31:32) sts on RH needle after cast-off. Turn and work on these sts for first side.

Dec 1 st at beg of the next row. Work 10 rows dec 1 st at neck edge on the 2 foll 4th rows, at the same time, dec 1 st at armhole edge on the next 4 rows and 3 foll alt rows. [16 (18:19:21:22) sts.]

This simple garment requires some skill when it comes to picking up stitches for the armholes.

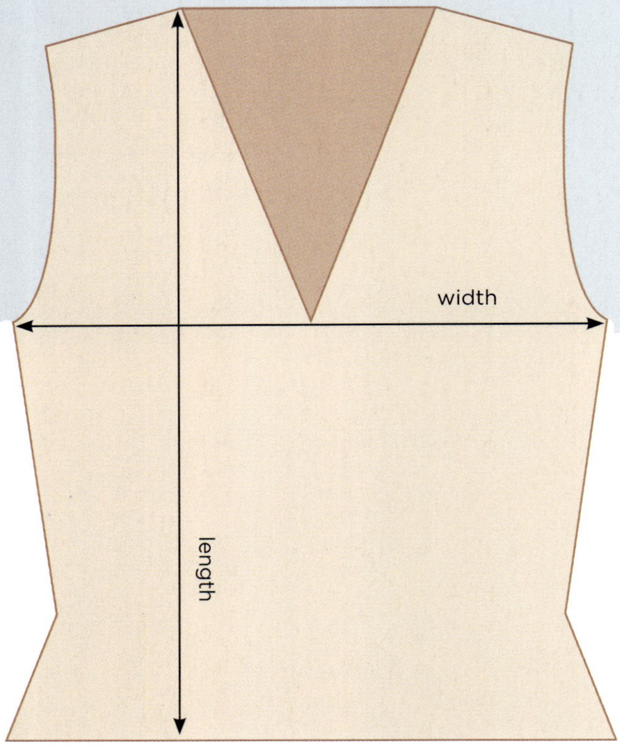

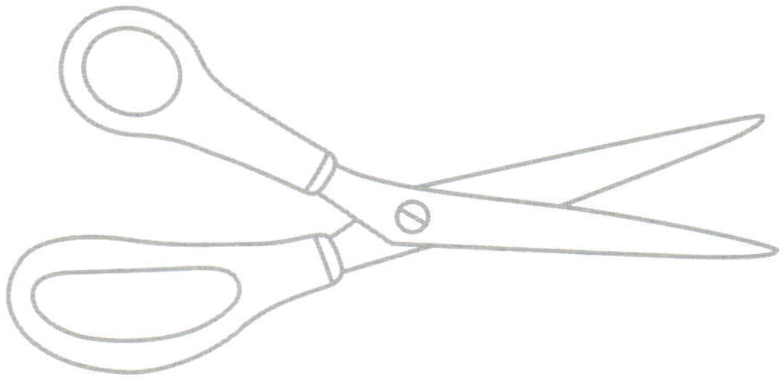

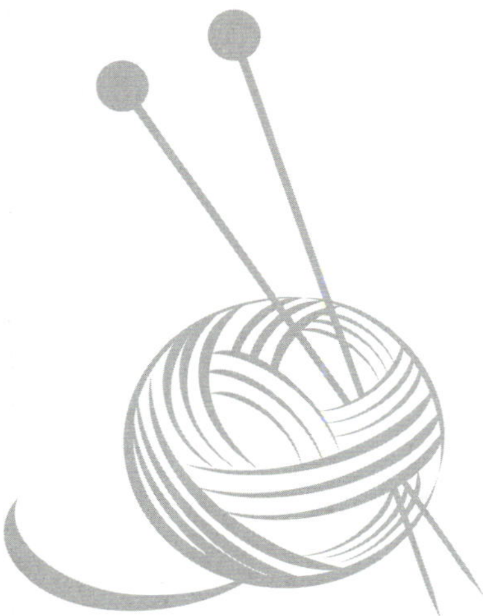

Keeping armhole edge straight, cont to dec 1 st at neck edge on every 4th row to 7 (9:9:11:11) sts, then work straight until Front matches Back to beg of shoulder shaping, ending with a WS row.

SHAPE SHOULDER

Cast off 3 (4:4:5:5) sts at beg of the next row. Work 1 row. Cast off rem 4 (5:5:6:6) sts.

With RS facing, slip the center st onto a safety pin (this marks the st), rejoin yarn and knit to end. Complete this side to match first side, reversing shapings.

NECKBAND

Join left shoulder. With RS facing, 4 mm needles and A, knit up 3 sts from right back neck, knit across 17 (17:19:19:21) sts from back neck st holder, dec 1 st in center of these sts, knit up 3 sts from left back neck, 35 (37:39:41:43) sts down left front neck, knit marked st, knit up 35 (37:39:41:43) sts up right front neck. [93 (97:103:107:113) sts.]

Next row: Beg with a 2nd rib row, rib to within 2 sts of marked st, p2tog, p1, p2tog-tbl, rib rem 55 (57:61:63:67) sts.

Next row: Rib to within 2 sts of marked st, k2tog-tbl, k1b, k2tog, rib to end.

Rib 3 more rows, dec either side of marked st as set. [83 (87:93:97:103) sts.] Cast off ribwise, dec as before.

ARMBANDS **(make 2)**

Join right shoulder and neckband.

With RS facing, 4 mm needles and A, knit up 81 (85:89:93:97) sts evenly along one armhole edge. Beg with a 2nd rib row, rib 5 rows. Cast off ribwise.

FINISHING

Join side seams.

Crochet basics

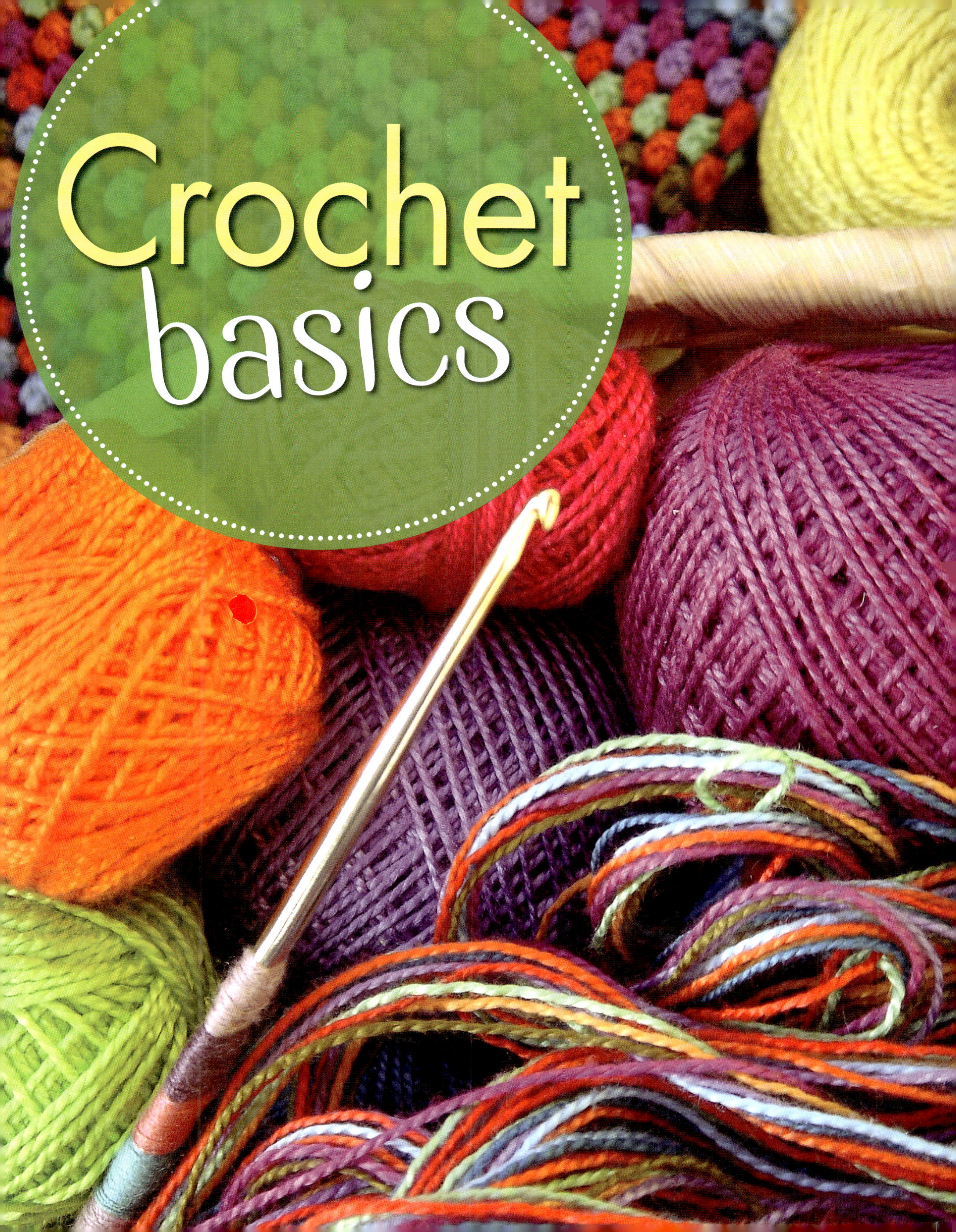

Basic Information

EQUIPMENT

Crochet is an incredibly versatile craft - you can achieve the most wonderful effects with the simplest of materials. All you really need is a crochet hook but you may find some other sewing essentials useful.

CROCHET HOOKS

The one essential piece of equipment you need to crochet is a crochet hook. The smallest size hooks are generally made of steel and come in sizes 0.60 mm to 2.50 mm. They are mostly used for delicate lace work using very fine yarns. Medium size hooks between 2.00 mm and 6.00 mm are usually made of coated aluminum or, in sizes 2.00 mm to 5.00 mm, bamboo. Large hooks in sizes 6.00 mm to 15.00 mm are made of plastic and may be hollow to reduce the weight. Old hooks may be bone, ivory, or Bakelite. Even if only one hook size is given in the instructions to make a garment, it's a good idea to buy the size above and the size below as well because you may need to change hook size to obtain the correct gauge (see page 52).

OTHER EQUIPMENT

As well as range of hooks, other items you'll need to make garments are a tape measure, markers, pins, a blunt-pointed sewing needle or a tapestry needle, and scissors.

YARNS

The projects use a wide range of yarns. Classic crochet uses smooth yarn and this is probably the best choice for a beginner as it is easier to see the stitches, but interesting effects can be obtained with the simplest of stitches and unusual, textured fashion yarns. Each project has been designed specifically for the yarn given in the instructions. This is not to say that the designs cannot be made using an alternative, but yarns vary so much that the you may not get the correct gauge, the amount of yarn you need to buy could be different, and the fabric you make may not behave in the same way as the original. Your choice could be a

CROCHET HOOK CONVERSION CHART APPROXIMATE SIZES

METRIC	AMERICAN	BRITISH
1.75 mm	5 or 6	15 or 2½ or 3
2.00 mm	1 or B	14 or 1½ or 1
2.50 mm	2 or C	12 or 0 or 2/0
3.00 mm	3 or D	10 or 11 sor 3/0
3.50 mm	4 or E	9
4.00 mm	5 or F	8
4.50 mm	6 or G	7
5.00 mm	8 or H	6
5.50 mm	9 or I	5
6.00 mm	10 or J	4
6.50 mm		3
7.00 mm	10½ or K	2
7.50 mm	11	1
8.00 mm	12	0
9.00 mm	15	000

triumph but it could be a disaster, so if you do use a different yarn, be prepared for a different result.

GETTING STARTED

FOLLOWING THE INSTRUCTIONS

Crochet instructions are really very easy to follow. Before you start to crochet your garment, read through the instructions and make sure you understand what to expect. Make sure that you have the right yarn and a selection of crochet hooks. Check that you know what measurements you are working to - the "to fit" sizes are provided as a guide, but it is always a good idea to check that you will be happy with the finished actual measurements, as the amount of movement room varies according to the design. If in doubt about which size to make, compare the actual measurements with a garment you already have and like. Where instructions for different sizes are given, figures are given for the smallest size first and the larger sizes, separated by colons, follow in brackets.

Abbreviations are used for many of the repetitive words that occur in crochet instructions. Here is a list of the most frequently used abbreviations; any additional abbreviations will be given with each individual pattern.

Square brackets are used where a set of instructions needs to be worked a number of times. For example: [3 tr in next ch sp] twice. This means that the instructions within the brackets are worked twice. Brackets can also be used to clarify working a group of stitches.

Stitch counts are also given at intervals throughout the pattern, often at the end of a row or round. These are set in square brackets.

Asterisks are used to indicate repetition of a sequence of instructions.

ABBREVIATIONS

beg	beginning
ch	chain
cont	continue
dc	double crochet
dec	decreas(e)(ing)
dtr	double treble
foll	following
htr	half treble
inc	increas(e)(ing)
patt	pattern
rep	repeat
RS	right side
sp(s)	space(s)
ss	slip stitch
st(s)	stitch(es)
tog	together
tr	treble
trtr	triple treble
WS	wrong side
yrh	yarn around hook

READING STITCH DIAGRAMS

Where appropriate, stitch diagrams are also given. The stitch diagrams conform to the international symbols, with a few variations to explain individual stitches. The diagrams should be read in rows or in rounds exactly as the crochet is worked. Each stitch is represented by a symbol placed to create a picture of the stitch pattern, although occasionally symbols will have been stretched or compressed for the sake of clarity. The purpose of the stitch diagrams is to provide a quick visual reference, as it is often a lot easier to recognize that five bars across a T mean wrap the yarn around the hook five times at the start of the stitch, rather than trying to remember what "quintr" means. However, the

STITCH CHART		
	UK	US
○	chain	chain
●	slip stitch	slip stitch
+	double crochet	single crochet
T	half treble	half double crochet
	treble	double crochet
	double treble	treble crochet
	triple treble	double treble crochet
	quadruple treble	
	quintuple treble	

written instructions are complete as they stand, and all the projects can be completed without the stitch diagrams. Each stitch diagram will have a key; the standard symbols for the basic stitches are listed above.

CHECKING YOUR GAUGE

Making sure that you have the correct gauge is extremely important as the finished item will look very different from the original if you don't get this right. Although each pattern states which hook size you should use, gauges can vary so it is intended as guide only. Always change the hook size and try again if you do not achieve the gauge given. Gauges in crochet seem to vary a great deal, probably because the stitch size is governed equally by the gauge of the yarn in your fingers and the size of the hook.

The stitches at the edge can distort, so the best way to check your gauge is to work a few more stitches and rows than given for a 4-in. (10-cm) square, then to count and mark the number of stitches and rows needed. Measure between markers or long pins. If you get more than 4 in. (10 cm), your crochet is too loose. Try again using a smaller hook. If you get less than 4 in. (10 cm), your work is too tight. Try again using a larger hook.

BASIC TECHNIQUES

MAKING A SLIP KNOT

Most projects start with a slip knot.

Make a loop in the yarn, near the end. Insert the hook, catch the yarn, and pull a loop through. Pull gently on both ends to tighten the knot and to close the loop on the hook.

HOLDING THE HOOK

Most hooks have a flattened area a little way down from the hooked end, which helps you to find the best place for your fingers and makes the hook more comfortable to hold. You can hold the hook like a pencil with the rounded end above your hand or like a knife with the end under your hand. Most people find the pencil grip more flexible but experiment to find which suits you. However you hold the hook, your grip should be light so you can easily extend the hook in a forward and back motion.

HOLDING THE YARN AND THE WORK

Hold the tail end of yarn from the slip knot between first finger and thumb of your left hand. As the work grows, move the work to keep the thumb and first finger grip near the place that a new stitch will be made. The yarn lies over the middle and third fingers and is then wrapped around the little finger to gauge it. For extra control, to tighten a loose gauge, or if working with fine or slippery yarns, wrap the yarn around the middle finger as well. Extending the middle finger lifts the yarn and makes it easy to catch the yarn with the hook.

CHAIN STITCH (ch)

Chain stitch may be used as a foundation for other stitches, to make spaces or arches between stitches, or to reach the height of the other stitches when working in rounds or turning and working in rows.

With a slip knot on the hook, take the hook in front of the yarn, dip the tip to take the yarn over the hook from back to front, and draw a new loop through the loop on the hook. Repeat for each chain stitch.

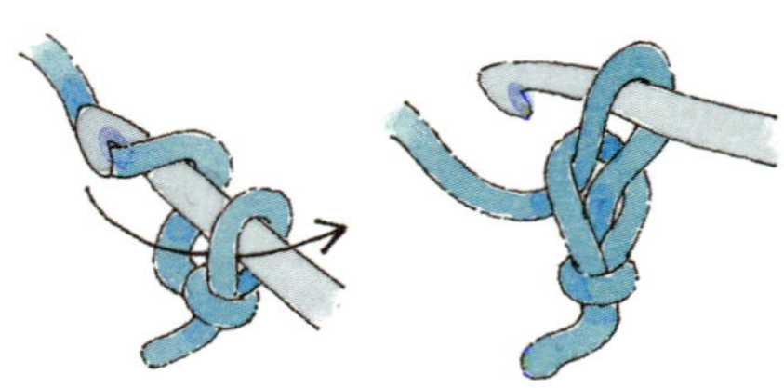

Here's a guide to the number of turning chain usually needed to give the correct height for some of the most often used stitches.

Double crochet	1 chain
Half treble	2 chains
Treble	3 chains
Double treble	4 chains

SLIP STITCH (ss)

Slip stitch is the shortest stitch. It's used mostly for joining stitches or to carry the yarn along an edge when shaping or to a new place in the stitch pattern to avoid having to break off and rejoin the yarn.

Insert hook into stitch, dip the tip of the hook to wrap the yarn over from back to front, and draw a new loop through both the stitch and the loop on the hook, so ending with one loop on the hook. The steps show joining a length of chain in a ring but the action is the same when working into any stitch.

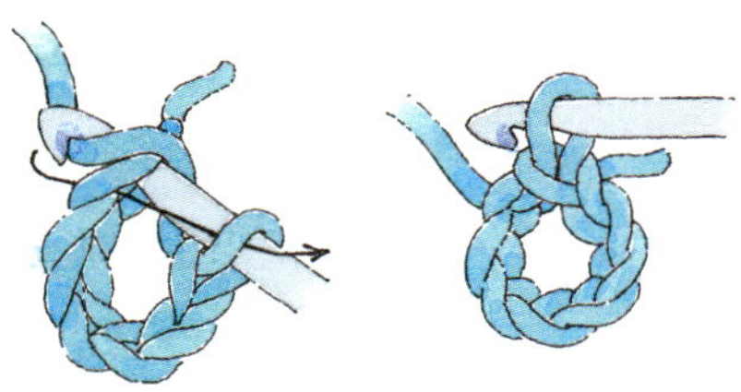

DOUBLE CROCHET (dc)

Double crochet is like a slip stitch with an extra step. Depending on the yarn and hook size used, it can make a firm fabric when used alone. Double crochet can also be used with other stitches to link chains or to create stitch patterns. In this book, a single chain is worked at the start of each double crochet row, but this chain is not worked into on the following row and it is not counted as a stitch. Some interesting variations on double crochet are Solomon's knot, crab stitch, and loop stitch.

Insert hook into chain or stitch indicated in the instructions, dip the tip of the hook to wrap the yarn around from back to front and draw the yarn through the stitch to make two loops on hook. Dip the tip of the hook to wrap the yarn around from back to front and draw the yarn through the two loops on the hook, ending with one loop on the hook.

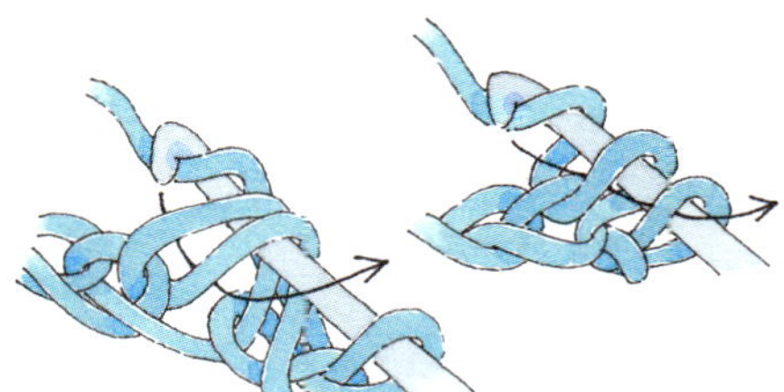

TREBLE CROCHET (tr)

Treble is like double crochet but with an extra step. It is probably the most frequently used stitch; when used alone it makes a light, flexible fabric and can be combined with other stitches in groups, fans, clusters, mesh, and openwork effects. Treble rows usually start with three chain to bring the yarn up to the height of the row, this counts as a stitch and the first stitch of the previous row is missed to compensate. However, this can leave a gap between the first and second stitches, so depending on the design, often the first chain is replaced with a double crochet worked directly into the first stitch.

With the hook in front of the yarn, dip the tip of the hook to wrap the yarn around from back to front. Insert hook into chain or stitch indicated in the instructions, dip the tip of the hook to wrap the yarn around from back to front, and draw the yarn through the stitch to make three loops on the hook. Dip the tip of the hook to wrap the yarn around from back to front and draw the yarn through the first two loops on the hook, wrap the yarn around the hook again, and draw it through the two loops, ending with one loop on the hook.

A half treble (htr) is worked in the same way as a treble up to the second step illustrated left, then the yarn is pulled through the new loop, the wrapped yarn, and the original loop all in one movement to make a stitch that's between double crochet and treble in height.

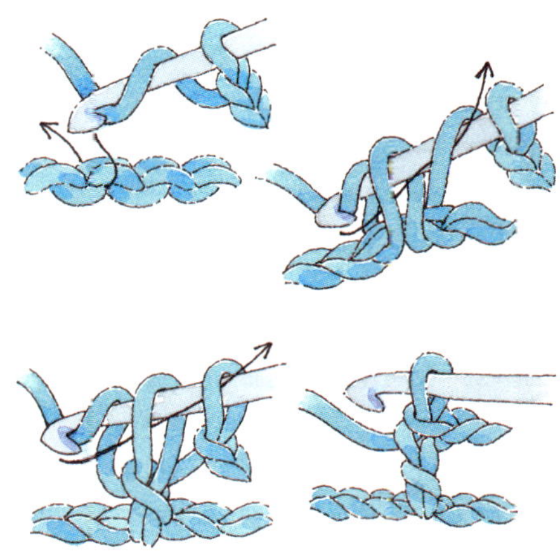

TIPS

- When working into the base chain, take the hook under two strands of each chain loop unless instructed otherwise.
- Wherever possible, join in new yarn at the start of a row, using the same method as changing colors.
- Try to work your base chain stitches quite loosely. If they are tight it will be difficult to work into them and the edge will pull in. To work an even, loose chain, try using a hook that is one or two sizes larger.

WORKING LONGER STITCHES

Double treble (dtr), triple treble (trtr), quadruple treble (quadtr), and quintuple treble (quintr) are all worked in the same way as a treble, but the stitches are made longer with one more wrapping of the yarn around the hook before you start, giving one more step when drawing through the loops at the end. The symbols show an extra bar for each time you wrap the yarn around the hook. Different height stitches are often combined to create a petal shape.

Here's a guide for the number of times to wrap the yarn around the hook when making longer stitches.

Double treble	twice
Triple treble	three times
Quadruple treble	four times
Quintuple treble	five times

VARIATIONS ON STANDARD STITCHES

INSERTING THE HOOK

All the standard stitches are worked either under two strands of the starting chain or under both strands at the top of a stitch but there are variations in placing the hook which give different effects.

Inserting the hook into one strand only

This can be either at the front or at the back of the stitch. This can be used practically, when working into both sides of a starting chain or decoratively, to open up a fabric.

Inserting the hook between stitches

This opens up the fabric and may be quicker to work. It can be used if the fabric is too fine or firm to insert the hook in the usual way or it can be used to group more stitches than would fit comfortably in a normal stitch.

Taking the hook around the stem of a stitch

This is called a raised stitch because it lies on the surface of the work. Prepare to make the stitch by wrapping the yarn around the hook as directed, take the hook in front of the work, and insert it down before the stitch designated in the row below, then up after the stitch, complete the stitch in the usual way. Raised stitches can also be made on the back of the work.

Inserting the hook in the side of a stitch

This is particularly useful when making a double or a treble chain. For a double chain, make a slip knot and two chains. Insert hook in first chain and work one double crochet stitch. For each following stitch, insert hook under the threads at the side of the previous stitch. For a treble chain, make a slip knot and three chains. Take the yarn around the hook, then insert hook in third chain, and complete the treble in the usual way. For each following stitch, insert the hook under one or two of the strands at the bottom of the previous stitch. Double and treble chains make a more flexible edge than an ordinary starting chain; they are also easier to count.

VARIATIONS ON DOUBLE CROCHET

SOLOMON'S KNOT

This stitch is simply a chain stitch, elongated and secured with a double crochet stitch.

Pull up loop to length required, take the yarn around the hook and pull through, making a loose chain stitch. Insert hook in the back loop of the chain and work a double crochet stitch; this will lock the loose chain in place.

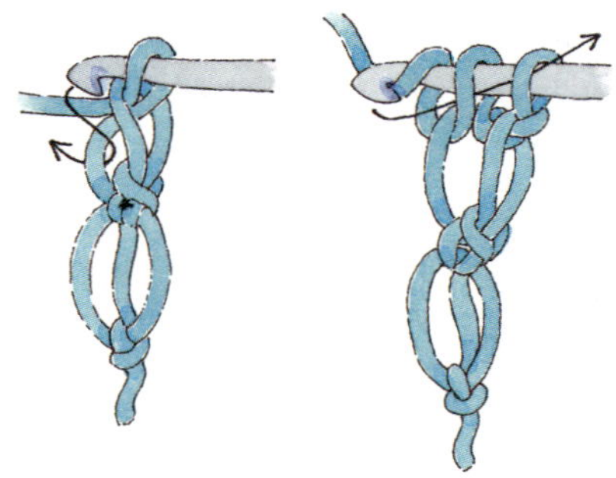

CRAB STITCH

This is an excellent edging stitch. It is literally double crochet, worked backward. It is best worked after a right side row of double crochet.

Do not turn the work at the end of the row. Insert the hook in the previous stitch, take the yarn around the hook and pull through to make two loops on the hook. Take the yarn around the hook again and pull through so one loop is left on the hook. Repeat along

the edge. Crab stitch spreads the edge slightly so there's no need to increase to turn a corner. If the edge flutes, either skip the occasional stitch in the double crochet row or use a smaller hook.

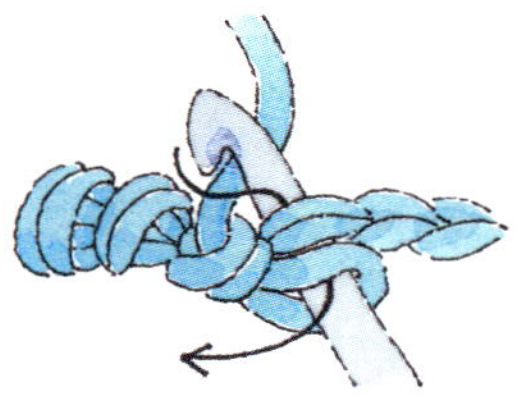

LOOP STITCH

This is really a double crochet stitch with the middle loop pulled out and locked with another stitch. It's always worked on wrong side rows, so the loop, which is made at the back of the work, is on the right side.

Insert hook. Extend middle finger to form a loop, take both threads of the loop around the hook, and pull through to make three loops on the hook. Take the yarn around the hook, pull through the three loops on the hook, and remove finger from loop. Keeping the middle finger of the left hand extended can be quite tiring; you may find it easier to transfer the extended loop to the middle finger of the right hand after pulling through to make three loops on the hook.

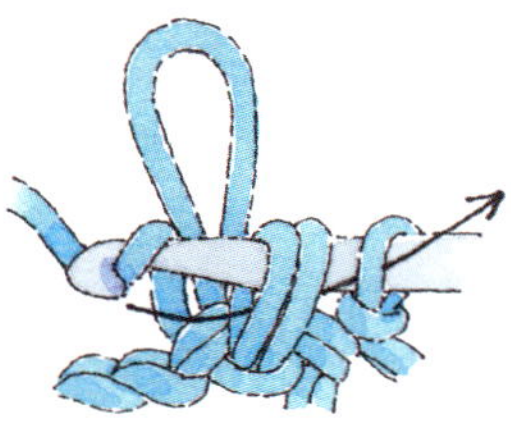

GROUPING STITCHES

Stitches of any length can be grouped or worked together to increase or decrease the number of stitches in a row or for a decorative effect. If complete stitches are worked into the same stitch, a fan or increase is made, or they can be linked at the top to give a popcorn. If the stitches are worked in a row but joined at the top, a cluster or decrease is made. Working stitches all in the same place and joining them at the top makes a bobble.

FAN / INCREASE

Working two or more complete stitches into the same stitch in the row below can increase the number of stitches in a row or be used to make a fan stitch pattern.

This example shows three treble stitches all worked into one treble in the row below. Simply work the trebles in the usual way but inserting the hook in the same stitch each time. Because the stitches are held together at the bottom but not at the top, working more than two or three stitches in the same place will give a fan shape.

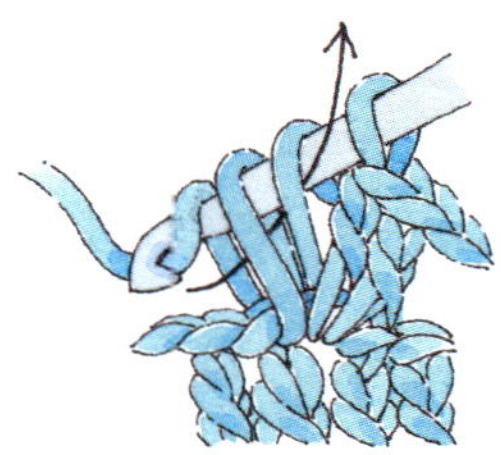

CLUSTER / DECREASE

Any combination of stitches can be joined together at the top by leaving the last loop of each stitch on the hook, then working all the loops together to complete the cluster. Clustering two or three stitches together can also be a way of decreasing.

This example shows how three stitches can be clustered together. Leaving the last loop of each stitch on the hook, work a treble into each of the next three stitches, making four loops on the hook. Take the yarn around the hook and pull through all four loops to join the stitches together at the top.

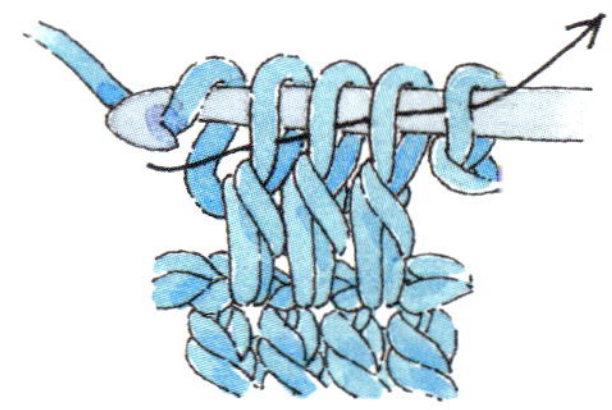

BOBBLE

When a cluster is worked into one stitch, a bobble is made. If the stitches used for the bobble are longer than the background stitches, the bobble will stand away from the surface.

This example shows three trebles worked together. Wrap the yarn around the hook and insert hook in stitch. Take the yarn around the hook and pull through. Do not complete the treble, leave this last loop on the hook and continue working part trebles, each time leaving one more loop on the hook, or in this case, until there are four loops on the hook including the original loop. Take the yarn around the hook and pull through all four loops.

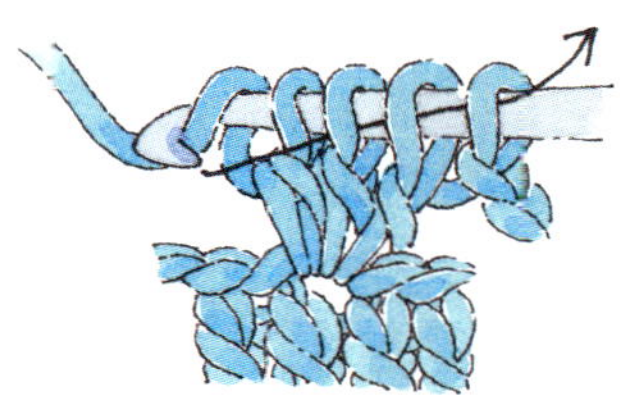

POPCORN

This method makes a bobble that stands up from the surface without the need to make longer stitches. A popcorn can be placed in any stitch and be made up of any practical number or combination of stitches.

Here a five-treble popcorn is worked into a chain space. Inserting hook in same place each time, work five complete trebles. Lengthen the last loop slightly and slip the hook out. Insert the hook into the top of the first stitch, then into the last loop. Take the yarn around the hook and pull through, tightening the stitch to make the popcorn stand up.

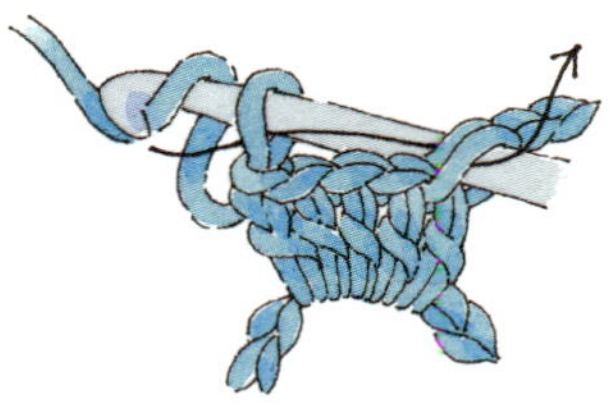

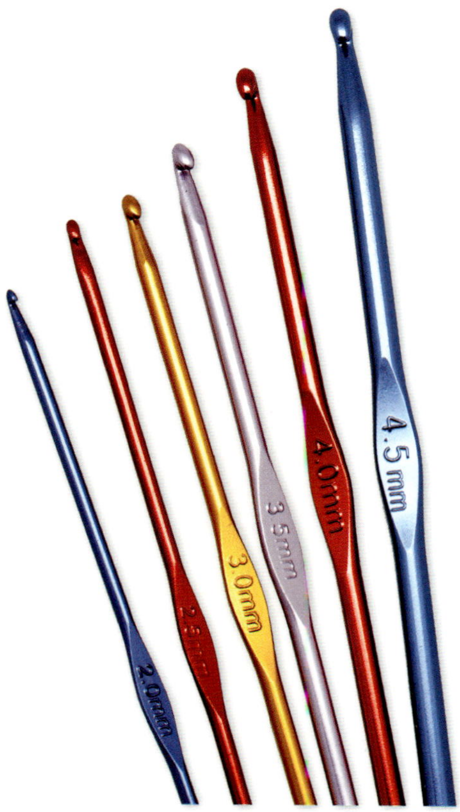

MAKING GARMENTS

WORKING IN ROWS

The fabric usually starts with a base chain, a double or treble chain, or a picot row. Each row of the instructions will tell you where to place the hook and which stitch to work. Simply turn the work at the end of each row so the right and the wrong side face alternately. The instructions will tell you how many turning chains to work or how to cope with the edge stitches.

WORKING IN ROUNDS

The fabric is worked from the center outward. The starting point can be a ring of chain or a loop ring. While chain gives a very firm start, loop rings can be neater and less obtrusive. A loop ring is made by working into yarn wound once around the left first finger, just like the first step in making a slip knot. The free end is worked over and pulled gently to close the ring when the first round of stitches has been completed.

When working in rounds, the right side always faces you. The instructions will tell you how to join at the end of each round and how many chain to work to match the height of the stitches in the next round.

COLOR CROCHET

Capital letters, A, B, C, etc. are used to designate the different colors. Because the last loop of a stitch forms the top of the next stitch, when changing colors, work the last stitch in the old color until two loops remain on the hook, then use the new color to complete the stitch. For some striped color patterns, you can carry the yarn not in use up the side of the work. If this is not practical, cut the yarn and work over the ends. When working color motifs, carry the yarn not in use along and slightly behind the top of the stitches in the row below and work over it until needed.

FINISHING GARMENTS

Some of the designs are worked in the round, so there is a minimum of finishing to do. Garments worked in flat pieces can be sewn together or joined with crochet. Placing markers and pinning seams will help to match the rows and give a neater finish. If sewing, preferably, join the pieces with the right sides facing, matching the rows and taking in two threads of each stitch from each side rather than whole stitches to reduce the bulk. Alternatively, place the right sides together and oversew the seams.

Joining a seam with crochet gives a firm, neat chain edge. Insert the hook under an edge stitch from each side and work a slip stitch or a double crochet stitch. The instructions will tell you if the crochet seams are intended to be decorative and should be worked with the right side facing. If the ball band allows the yarn to be pressed, press the pieces, checking that they are the correct size. Press again after joining the shoulders and setting in the sleeves.

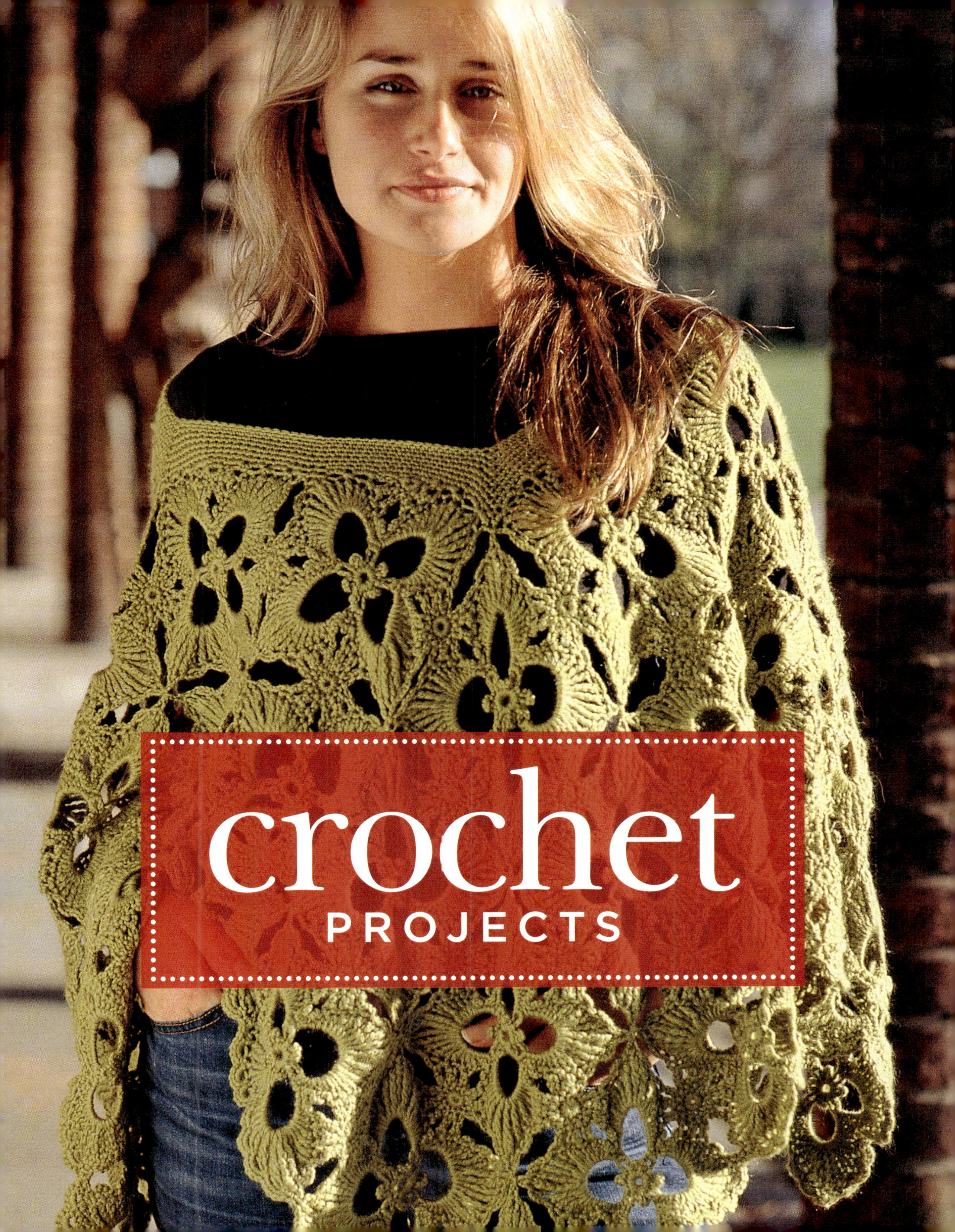
crochet
PROJECTS

shaded blanket coat

Worked mostly in treble crochet, this wrap over coat is designed to exploit the clever shaded effect of the lightweight bouclé yarn.

By Melody Griffiths, from her book *Simple Stylish Crochet*

BEGINNER

MEASUREMENTS

To fit bust

in.	32-34	36-38	40-42	44-46
cm	81-86	91-97	102-107	112-11

Actual width

in.	35	39¼	43½	47¾
cm	89	100	110.5	121.5

Actual length

in.	31½	32	32¾	33½
cm	80	81.5	83	85

Actual sleeve seam

19 in. (48 cm)

➤ In the instructions figures are given for the smallest size first; larger sizes follow in brackets. Where only one set of figures is given, this applies to all sizes.

MATERIALS

- 2 x 400 g balls of Sirdar Yo-Yo in Damson Mist 14
- 5.00 mm crochet hook

GAUGE

11 sts and 6 rows to 4 in. (10 cm) measured over treble stitch using 5.00 mm hook. Change hook size if necessary to obtain this gauge.

ABBREVIATIONS

2trtog - leaving last loop of each st on hook, work a treble in each of next 2 sts, yrh and pull through 3 loops on hook

See also page 51.

COAT

BACK AND FRONTS

Row 1: 3 ch, 1 dc in 1st ch, [4 ch, 1 dc in 3rd ch] 72 (78:84:90) times.

Row 2: (WS) 1 dc in 1st picot, 2 ch, [1 tr between picots, 1 tr in next picot] 72 (78:84:90) times. [145 (157:169:181) sts.]

Row 3: 1 dc in 1st tr, 2 ch, 1 tr in each tr to last st, 1 tr in 2nd ch.

Row 3 forms treble crochet. Cont in tr, work 17 more rows.

Dec row 1: (RS) 1 dc in 1st tr, 2 ch, 1 tr in each of next 33 (36:39:42) tr, [2trtog] 4 times, 1 tr in each of next 61 (67:73:79) tr, [2trtog] 4 times, 1 tr in each of next 33 (36:39:42) tr, 1 tr in 2nd ch. [137 (149:161:173) sts.]

Cont in tr, work 3 rows.

Dec row 2: 1 dc in 1st tr, 2 ch, 1 tr in each of next 31 (34:37:40) tr, [2trtog] 4 times, 1 tr in each of next 57 (63:69:75) tr, [2trtog] 4 times, 1 tr in each of next 31 (34:37:40) tr, 1 tr in 2nd ch. [129 (141:153:165) sts.]

Cont in tr, work 3 rows.

Dec row 3: 1 dc in 1st tr, 2 ch, 1 tr in each of next 29 (32:35:38) tr, [2trtog] 4 times, 1 tr in each of next 53 (59:65:71) tr, [2trtog] 4 times, 1 tr in each of next 29 (32:35:38) tr, 1 tr in 2nd ch. [121 (133:145:157) sts.]

Cont in tr, work 3 rows.

Dec row 4: 1 dc in 1st tr, 2 ch, 1 tr in each of next 27 (30:33:36) tr, [2trtog] 4 times, 1 tr in each of next 49 (55:61:67) tr, [2trtog] 4 times, 1 tr in each of next 27 (30:33:36) tr, 1 tr in 2nd ch. [113 (125:137:149) sts.]

Cont in tr, work 3 rows.

Dec row 5: 1 dc in 1st tr, 2 ch, 1 tr in each of next 25 (28:31:34) tr, [2trtog] 4 times, 1 tr in each of next 45 (51:57:63) tr, [2trtog] 4 times, 1 tr in each of next 25 (28:31:34) tr, 1 tr in 2nd ch. [105 (117:129:141) sts.]

Cont in tr, work one row.

Divide for armholes and shape collar

Row 1: (RS) 1 dc in 1st tr, 2 ch, 1 tr in same tr, 1 tr in each of next 25 (28:31:34) tr, fasten off and break yarn, miss 4 tr, join yarn in next tr, 3 ch, 1 tr in each of next 44 (50:56:62) tr, fasten off and break yarn, miss 4 tr, join yarn in next tr, 3 ch, 1 tr in each of next 24 (27:30:33) tr, 2 tr in 2nd ch. [27 (30:33:36) sts in each front and 45 (51:57:63) sts in back.]

Row 2: 1 dc in 1st tr, 2 ch, 1 tr in same tr, 1 tr in each of next 23 (26:29:32) tr, 2trtog, 1 tr in 3rd ch, fasten off

Use left over yarn to make a scarf.

It's easy to crochet with this textured yarn because the bouclé loops are too small and closely spaced to catch on the hook.

and break yarn, join yarn in 1st tr of back, 3 ch, 2trtog, 1 tr in each of next 39 (45:51:57) tr, 2trtog, 1 tr in 3rd ch, fasten off and break yarn, join yarn in 1st tr of right front, 3 ch, 2trtog, 1 tr in each of next 23 (26:29:32) tr, 2 tr in 2nd ch. [27 (30:33:36) sts in each front and 43 (49:55:61) sts in back.] Do not fasten off, leave back and fronts with yarn attached.

SLEEVES (make 2)

Make 15 (16:17:18) picots as given for back. Work Row 1 as given for back and fronts. [29 (31:33:35) sts.] Cont in tr as given for back, work 6 (6:2:2) rows.

Inc row: 1 dc in 1st tr, 2 ch, 1 tr in same tr, 1 tr in each tr to last st, 2 tr in 2nd ch. [31 (33:35:37) sts.]

Cont in tr, inc in this way at each end of 5 (5:6:6) foll 4th rows. [41 (43:47:49) sts.]

Work 1 row.

SHAPE TOP

Row 1: (RS) Ss in each of first 4 tr, 3 ch, 1 tr in each of next 34 (36:40:42) tr, turn and leave 3 sts. [35 (37:41:43) sts.]

Dec row: 1 dc in 1st tr, 2 ch, 2trtog, 1 tr in each of next 29 (31:35:37) tr, 2trtog, 1 tr in 3rd ch. [33 (35:39:41) sts.] Fasten off.

Helpful hint. When working the two rows to divide the back and fronts and shape the underarms, it's important to break and rejoin the yarn for each section to keep the continuity of the color shading.

YOKE

Row 1: (RS) Across 27 (30:33:36) sts of right front work 1 dc in 1st tr, 2 ch, 1 tr in same tr, 1 tr in each of next 22 (25:28:31) tr, [2trtog] twice, across 33 (35:39:41) sts of right sleeve work * [2trtog] twice, 1 tr in each of next 25 (27:31:33) tr, [2trtog] twice *, across 43 (49:55:61) sts of back work [2trtog] twice, 1 tr in each of next 35 (41:47:53) tr, [2trtog] twice, rep from * to * across 33 (35:39:41) sts of left sleeve, across 27 (30:33:36) sts of left front work [2trtog] twice, 1 tr in each of next 22 (25:28:31) tr, 2 tr in 2nd ch. [149 (165:185:201) sts.]

Row 2: 1 dc in 1st tr, 2 ch, 1 tr in same tr, 1 tr in each of next 21 (24:27:30) tr, [2trtog] 4 times, 1 tr in each of next 21 (23:27:29) tr, [2trtog] 4 times, 1 tr in each of next 31 (37:43:49) tr, [2trtog] 4 times, 1 tr in each of next 21 (23:27:29) tr, [2trtog] 4 times, 1 tr in each of next 21 (24:27:30) tr, 2 tr in 2nd ch. [135 (151:171:187) sts.]

Row 3: 1 dc in 1st tr, 2 ch, 1 tr in same tr, 1 tr in each of next 20 (23:26:29) tr, [2trtog] 4 times, 1 tr in each of next 17 (19:23:25) tr, [2trtog] 4 times, 1 tr in each of next 27 (33:39:45) tr, [2trtog] 4 times, 1 tr in each of next 17 (19:23:25) tr, [2trtog] 4 times, 1 tr in each of next 20 (23:26:29) tr, 2 tr in 2nd ch. [121 (137:157:173) sts.]

Row 4: 1 dc in 1st tr, 2 ch, 1 tr in same tr, 1 tr in each of next 19 (22:25:28) tr, [2trtog] 4 times, 1 tr in each of next 13 (15:19:21) tr, [2trtog] 4 times, 1 tr in each of next 23 (29:35:41) tr, [2trtog] 4 times, 1 tr in each of next 13 (15:19:21) tr, [2trtog] 4 times, 1 tr in each of next 19 (22:25:28) tr, 2 tr in 2nd ch. [107 (123:143:159) sts.]

Row 5: 1 dc in 1st tr, 2 ch, 1 tr in same tr, 1 tr in each of next 18 (21:24:27) tr, [2trtog] 4 times, 1 tr in each of next 9 (11:15:17) tr, [2trtog] 4 times, 1 tr in each of next 19 (25:31:37) tr, [2trtog] 4 times, 1 tr in each of next 9 (11:15:17) tr, [2trtog] 4 times, 1 tr in each of next 18 (21:24:27) tr, 2 tr in 2nd ch. [93 (109:129:145) sts.]

Row 6: 1 dc in 1st tr, 2 ch, 1 tr in same tr, 1 tr in each of next 17 (20:23:26) tr, [2trtog] 4 times, 1 tr in each of next 5 (7:11:13) tr, [2trtog] 4 times, 1 tr in each of next 15 (21:27:33) tr, [2trtog] 4 times, 1 tr in each of next 5 (7:11:13) tr, [2trtog] 4 times, 1 tr in each of next 17 (20:23:26) tr, 2 tr in 2nd ch. [79 (95:115:131) sts.]

2nd size only

Row 7: 1 dc in 1st tr, 2 ch, 1 tr in same tr, 1 tr in each of next 19 tr, [2trtog] 3 times, 1 tr in each of next 7 tr, [2trtog] 3 times, 1 tr in each of next 17 tr, [2trtog] 3 times, 1 tr in each of next 7

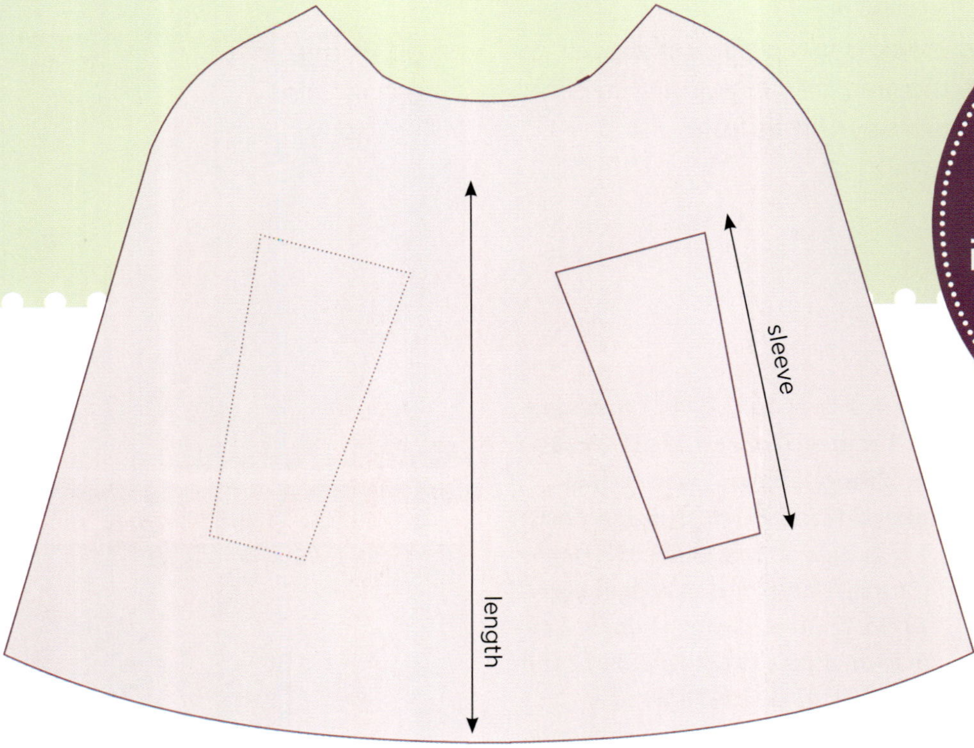

The picot edging is not just decorative; in this yarn it is easier to work into and between picots than to find the loops of a starting chain.

tr, [2trtog] 3 times, 1 tr in each of next 19 tr, 2 tr in 2nd ch. [85 sts.]

3rd size only

Row 7: 1 dc in 1st tr, 2 ch, 1 tr in same tr, 1 tr in each of next 22 tr, [2trtog] 4 times, 1 tr in each of next 7 tr, [2trtog] 4 times, 1 tr in each of next 22 tr, [2trtog] 4 times, 1 tr in each of next 7 tr, [2trtog] 4 times, 1 tr in each of next 22 tr, 2 tr in 2nd ch. [101 sts.]

Row 8: 1 dc in 1st tr, 2 ch, 1 tr in same tr, 1 tr in each of next 21 tr, [2trtog] 3 times, 1 tr in each of next 7 tr, [2trtog] 3 times, 1 tr in each of next 19 tr, [2trtog] 3 times, 1 tr in each of next 7 tr, [2trtog] 3 times, 1 tr in each of next 21 tr, 2 tr in 2nd ch. [91 sts.]

4th size only

Row 7: 1 dc in 1st tr, 2 ch, 1 tr in same tr, 1 tr in each of next 25 tr, [2trtog] 4 times, 1 tr in each of next 9 tr, [2trtog] 4 times, 1 tr in each of next 29 tr, [2trtog] 4 times, 1 tr in each of next 9 tr, [2trtog] 4 times, 1 tr in each of next 25 tr, 2 tr in 2nd ch. [117 sts.]

Row 8: 1 dc in 1st tr, 2 ch, 1tr in same tr, 1 tr in each of next 24 tr, [2trtog] 3 times, 1 tr in each of next 9 tr, [2trtog] 3 times, 1 tr in each of next 25 tr, [2trtog] 3 times, 1 tr in each of next 9 tr, [2trtog] 3 times, 1 tr in each of next 24 tr, 2tr in 2nd ch. [107 sts.]

Row 9: 1 dc in 1st tr, 2 ch, 1 tr in same tr, 1 tr in each of next 23 tr, [2trtog] 3 times, 1 tr in each of next 7 tr, [2trtog] 3 times, 1 tr in each of next 21 tr, [2trtog] 3 times, 1 tr in each of next 7 tr, [2trtog] 3 times, 1 tr in each of next 23 tr, 2tr in 2nd ch. [97 sts.]

All sizes

[79 (85:91:97) sts.] Incs at front edges for collar have been completed.

Helpful hint. The back and fronts of the coat are worked in one to the armholes so the shading in the yarn flows around the body. The shading on the sleeves is wider than the color stripes on the body because the rows are shorter.

Next row: 1 dc in 1st tr, 2 ch, 1 tr in each of next 18 (20:22:24) tr, [2trtog] twice, 1 tr in each of next 5 tr, [2trtog] twice, 1 tr in each of next 15 (17:19:21) tr, [2trtog] twice, 1 tr in each of next 5 tr, [2trtog] twice, 1 tr in each of next 18 (20:22:24) tr, 1 tr in 2nd ch. [71 (77:83:89) sts.]

Next row: 1 dc in 1st tr, 2 ch, 1 tr in each of next 17 (19:21:23) tr, [2trtog] twice, 1 tr in each of next 3 tr, [2trtog] twice, 1 tr in each of next 13 (15:17:19) tr, [2trtog] twice, 1 tr in each of next 3 tr, [2trtog] twice, 1 tr in each of next 17 (19:21:23) tr, 1 tr in 2nd ch. [63 (69:75:81) sts.]

Next row: 1 dc in 1st tr, 2 ch, 1 tr in each of next 16 (18:20:22) tr, [2trtog] twice, 1 tr in next tr, [2trtog] twice, 1 tr in each of next 11 (13:15:17) tr, [2trtog] twice, 1 tr in next tr, [2trtog] twice, 1 tr in each of next 16 (18:20:22) tr, 1 tr in 2nd ch. [55 (61:67:73) sts.]

Cont in tr, work 11 rows. Fasten off.

EDGING

With WS facing, join yarn at lower edge of left front. Spacing picots evenly, work up left front edge, along collar edge and down right front edge.

Picot row: 1 dc, 3 ch, ss in side of last dc, [2dc, 3ch, ss in side of last dc] to end.

TIE BELT (optional)

Make 65 (66:67:68) picots and work Row 1 as given for back and fronts. Work picot row as given for edging into Row 1. Fasten off.

FINISHING

Taking one st from each edge into seam, join sleeve seams. Join underarm seams. Try on coat and mark position for belt loops. Make a loop of crochet chain for each belt loop.

lacy scarves

Combine a lacy stitch with luxury yarn to make these cozy scarves. Choose either the fluffy version for casual wear, or the sophisticated shorter version in silk for a smarter look.

By Sue Whiting, from her book *Learn to Crochet*

BEGINNER

MEASUREMENTS

Long scarf is approx 8½ in. (22 cm) wide and 71 in. (180 cm) long (excluding fringe)

Short scarf is approx 8 in. (20 cm) wide and 45¼ in. (115 cm) long

MATERIALS

For the long scarf:

- 4 x 50 g balls of Rowan Kid Soft in magenta
- 5.00 mm (USA H8/ UK 6) crochet hook

For the short scarf:

- 3 x 50 g balls of Jaeger Silk 4 ply in purple
- 2.50 mm (USA C2/UK 12) crochet hook

GAUGE

Long scarf (shown in pink): 4 patt repeats (16 sts) to 4¼ in. (11 cm) and 12 rows to 4½ in. (12 cm) using 5.00 mm hook, or size required to give correct gauge.

Short scarf (shown in purple): 9 patt repeats (36 sts) to 5 in. (13 cm) and 16 rows to 6 in. (15 cm) using 2.50 mm hook, or size required to give correct gauge.

ABBREVIATIONS

cluster - *yoh and insert hook as indicated, yoh and draw loop through lengthening loop to approx 10mm for long scarf or 7mm for short scarf, yoh and draw through 2 loops on hook, rep from * once more, yoh and draw through 2 loops on hook, yoh and draw through last 2 loops on hook.

See also page 51.

LONG SCARF

Using 5.00 mm hook, make 35 ch.

Foundation row: Miss 4 ch (counts as 1 tr and 1 ch), *(1 cluster, 2 ch and 1 cluster) into next ch, miss 3 ch, rep from * to last 3 ch, (1 cluster, 2 ch and 1 cluster) into next ch, miss 1 ch, 1 tr into last ch, turn. 8 patt repeats, 34 sts.

Now work in patt as follows:

Row 1: 3 ch (counts as 1 tr), (1 tr, 2 ch and 1 tr) into each ch sp to end, 1 tr into top of turning ch, turn.

Row 2: 3 ch (counts as 1 tr), (1 cluster, 2 ch and 1 cluster) into each ch sp to end, 1 tr into top of turning ch, turn.

Rows 1 and 2 form patt.

Cont in patt until scarf measures 71 in. (180 cm), ending after patt row 2.

Fasten off.

For fringe, cut 12 in. (30 cm) lengths of yarn and knot pairs of threads across short ends of scarf, positioning each knot of fringe in corners of scarf and between each pair of clusters.

Do not press.

SHORT SCARF

Using 2.50 mm hook, make 59 ch.

Work foundation row as for Long Scarf. 14 patt repeats, 58 sts.

Beg with patt row 1, work in patt as for Long Scarf until work measures 45¼ in. (115 cm), ending after patt row 2.

Do NOT fasten off.

Edging round: Working down adjacent row end edge, work 3 ch, 1 dc around tr at end of last row, *3 ch, 1 dc around 3 ch at beg of previous row, 3 ch, 1 dc around tr at end of previous row, rep from * until dc has been worked around tr at end of foundation row, 3 ch, 1 dc into same place as last dc, now working across foundation ch edge, work *3 ch, miss ch at base of clusters, (1 dc, 3 ch and 1 dc) into next ch sp, rep from * until both dc have been worked into ch sp at beg of foundation row, cont in this way until all four edges have been completed, replacing "dc" at end of last rep with "ss to first dc".

Fasten off.

Press lightly.

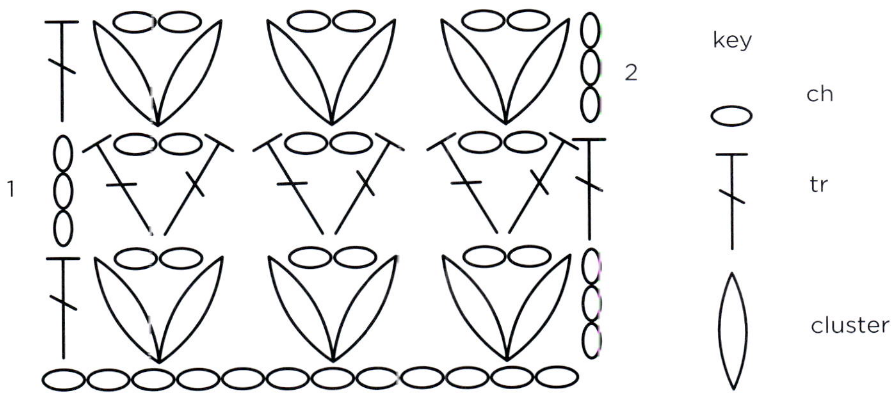

➤ This stitch diagram shows the stitches used for both scarves.

cardigan with frilled edge

This soft, supple cashmere mix yarn is a joy to handle and gives an exquisite quality to the easy-to-work, double and treble stitch pattern used for this sophisticated but simple cardigan.

By Melody Griffiths, from her book *Simple Stylish Crochet*

BEGINNER

MEASUREMENTS

To fit bust

in.	32	34	36	38	40	42	44
cm	81	86	91	97	102	107	112

Actual bust

in.	35	37½	39¾	42	44½	47¼	49½
cm	89	95	101	107	113	120	126

Actual length

in.	24	24	24½	24½	25¼	25¼	26
cm	60.5	60.5	62.5	62.5	64.5	64.5	66

Actual sleeve

19 in. (48 cm)

➤ In the instructions figures are given for the smallest size first; larger sizes follow in brackets. Where only one set of figures is given, this applies to all sizes.

MATERIALS

- 15 (16:16:17:18:18:19) x 50 g balls of Debbie Bliss Cashmerino Aran in 101
- 5.00 mm crochet hook

➤ Work the starting chain loosely; if necessary, use one size larger hook.

GAUGE

13 sts and 11 rows to 4 in. (10 cm) measured over double crochet and treble pattern using 5.00 mm hook. Change hook size if necessary to obtain this gauge.

➤ Instead of the usual 3 ch, a dc and 2 ch is worked at the start of each treble row to close the gap between the first and second stitches. Stretch the loop on the hook slightly before making the dc.

➤ The 1 ch at the start of a dc row does not count as a stitch.

ABBREVIATIONS

3trtog - leaving last loop of each st on hook, work a treble in each of next 3 sts, yrh and pull through 4 loops on hook

See also page 51.

CARDIGAN

BACK

Make 51 (55:59:63:67:71:75) ch.

Row 1: (WS) 1 dc in 2nd ch from hook, 1 dc in each ch to end. [50 (54:58:62:66:70:74) sts.]

Row 2: 1 dc in 1st dc, 2 ch, 1 tr in each dc to end.

Row 3: 1 ch, 1 dc in each tr to last st, 1dc in 2nd ch.

Rows 2 and 3 form dc and tr patt. Cont in patt, work 20 more rows, ending with a 3rd patt row.

Inc row: (RS) 1 dc in 1st dc, 2 ch, 1 tr in 1st dc, 1 tr in each dc to last dc, 2 tr in last dc. [52 (56:60:64:68:72:76) sts.]

Cont in patt, inc in this way at each end of 3 foll 6th rows. [58 (62:66:70:74:78:82) sts.]

Cont in patt, work 3 rows, ending with a 3rd patt row.

SHAPE ARMHOLES

Next row: (RS) Ss in each of first 3 (3:4:4:5:5:6) dc, 3 ch, miss dc with ss, 1 tr in each dc to last 2 (2:3:3:4:4:5) dc, turn.

[54 (58:60:64:66:70:72) sts.] Patt 1 row.

Dec row: 1 dc in first dc, 2 ch, 3trtog, 1 tr in each dc to last 4 sts, 3trtog, 1 tr in last dc. [50 (54:56:60:62:66:68) sts.]

Patt 1 row. Work dec row again. [46 (50:52:56:58:62:64) sts.]

Patt 1 row. Work dec row again. [42 (46:48:52:54:58:60) sts.] Patt 15 (15:17:17:19:19:21) rows, ending with a 3rd patt row. Fasten off.

LEFT FRONT

Make 33 (35:37:39:41:43:45) ch.

Row 1: (WS) 1 dc in 2nd ch from hook, 1 dc in each ch to end. [32 (34:36:38:40:42:44) sts.]

Row 2: 1 dc in 1st dc, 2 ch, 1 tr in each dc to end.

Row 3: 1 ch, 1 dc in each tr to last st, 1 dc in 2nd ch.

Rows 2 and 3 form dc and tr patt. Cont in patt, work 20 more rows, ending with a 3rd patt row **.

Inc row: (RS) 1 dc in 1st dc, 2 ch, 1 tr in 1st dc, 1 tr in each dc to end. [33 (35:37:39:41:43:45) sts.]

Cont in patt, inc in this way at beg of 3 foll 6th rows. [36 (38:40:42:44:46:48) sts.] Cont in patt, work 3 rows, ending with a 3rd patt row.

SHAPE ARMHOLE

Next row: (RS) Ss in each of first 3 (3:4:4:5:5:6) dc, 3 ch, miss dc with ss, 1 tr in each dc to end. [34 (36:37:39:40:42:43) sts.] Patt 1 row.

Dec row: 1 dc in first dc, 2 ch, 3trtog, 1 tr in each dc to end. [32 (34:35:37:38:40:41) sts.]

Patt 1 row. Work dec row again. [30 (32:33:35:36:38:39) sts.]

Patt 1 row. Work dec row again. [28 (30:31:33:34:36:37) sts.]

Patt 9 (9:11:11:13:13:15) rows, ending with a 3rd patt row.

SHAPE NECK

Row 1: (RS) 1 dc in 1st dc, 2 ch, 1 tr in each of next 8 (10:11:12:13:14:15) dc, 3trtog, 1 tr in next dc, turn and leave 15 (15:15:16:16:17:17) dc for neck. [11 (13:14:15:16:17:18) sts.] Patt 1 row.

Row 3: 1 dc in 1st dc, 2 ch, 1 tr in each dc to last 4 dc, 3trtog, 1 tr in last dc. [9 (11:12:13: 14:15:16) sts.] Patt 3 rows. Fasten off.

RIGHT FRONT

Work as given for Left Front to **.

Inc row: (RS) 1 dc in 1st dc, 2 ch, 1 tr in each dc to last dc, 2 tr in last dc. [33 (35:37:39:41:43:45) sts.] Cont in patt, inc in this way at end of 3 foll 6th rows. [36 (38:40:42:44:46:48) sts.] Cont in patt, work 3 rows, ending with a 3rd patt row.

Variation. If you'd like just a small shell edging, finish the fronts and neck edge with Row 1 and Row 6 of front and neck edging as given for the cuffs. If you do this, you'll need one less ball of yarn.

SHAPE ARMHOLE

Next row: (RS) 1 dc in 1st dc, 2 ch, 1 tr in each dc to last 2 (2:3:3:4:4:5) dc, turn. [34 (36:37:39:40:42:43) sts.] Patt 1 row.

Dec row: (RS) 1 dc in first dc, 2 ch, 1 tr in each dc to last 4 sts, 3trtog, 1 tr in last dc. [32 (34:35:37:38:40:41) sts.]

Patt 1 row. Work dec row again. [30 (32:33:35:36:38:39) sts.]

Patt 1 row. Work dec row again. [28 (30:31:33:34:36:37) sts.]

Patt 9 (9:11:11:13:13:15) rows, ending with a 3rd patt row. Fasten off. With RS facing, leave first 15 (15:15:16:16:17:17) dc for neck.

SHAPE NECK

Row 1: (RS) Join yarn and work 1 dc in next dc, 2 ch, 3trtog, 1 tr in each dc to end. [11 (13:14:15:16:17:18) sts.] Patt 1 row.

Row 3: 1 dc in 1st dc, 2 ch, 3trtog, 1 tr in each dc to end. [9 (11:12:13:14:15:16) sts.]

Patt 3 rows. Fasten off.

SLEEVES (make 2)

Make 31 (31:31:35:35:39:39) ch.

Row 1: (WS) 1 dc in 2nd ch from hook, 1 dc in each ch to end.

[30 (30:30:34:34:38:38) sts.] Work in dc and tr patt as given for back for 4 rows.

Cont in patt, inc in same way as back at each end of next row and on 6 (7:7:7:7:7:7) foll 6th rows. [44 (46:46:50:50:54:54) sts.]

Inc at each end of next 0 (0:1:0:1:0:2) RS rows. [44 (46:48:50:52:54:58) sts.]

Patt 11 (5:3:5:3:5:1) rows.

SHAPE TOP

Next row: (RS) Ss in each of first 3 (3:4:4:5:5:6) dc, 3 ch, miss dc with ss, 1 tr in each dc to last 2 (2:3:3:4:4:5) dc, turn.

[40 (42:42:44:44:46:48) sts.] Patt 1 row.

Dec row: 1 dc in first dc, 2 ch, 3trtog, 1 tr in each dc to last 4 sts, 3trtog, 1 tr in last dc. [36 (38:38:40:40:42:44) sts.]

Dec in this way at each end of next 6 RS rows. [12 (14:14:16:16:18:20) sts.]

Patt 1 (1:3:1:3:1:3) rows. Fasten off.

EDGINGS

PREPARATION FOR FRONT AND NECK EDGING

Matching sts, join shoulders. With WS facing, work 87 (87:91:91:95:95:99) dc up left front edge to start of neck shaping. Fasten off. Starting at neck edge, work 86 (86:90:90:94:94:98) dc along right front edge. Fasten off. With WS of left front facing, join yarn after 15 (15:15:16:16:17:17) dc at neck and work 9 dc around shaped edge to shoulder. Fasten off. Starting at shoulder, work right front neck to match.

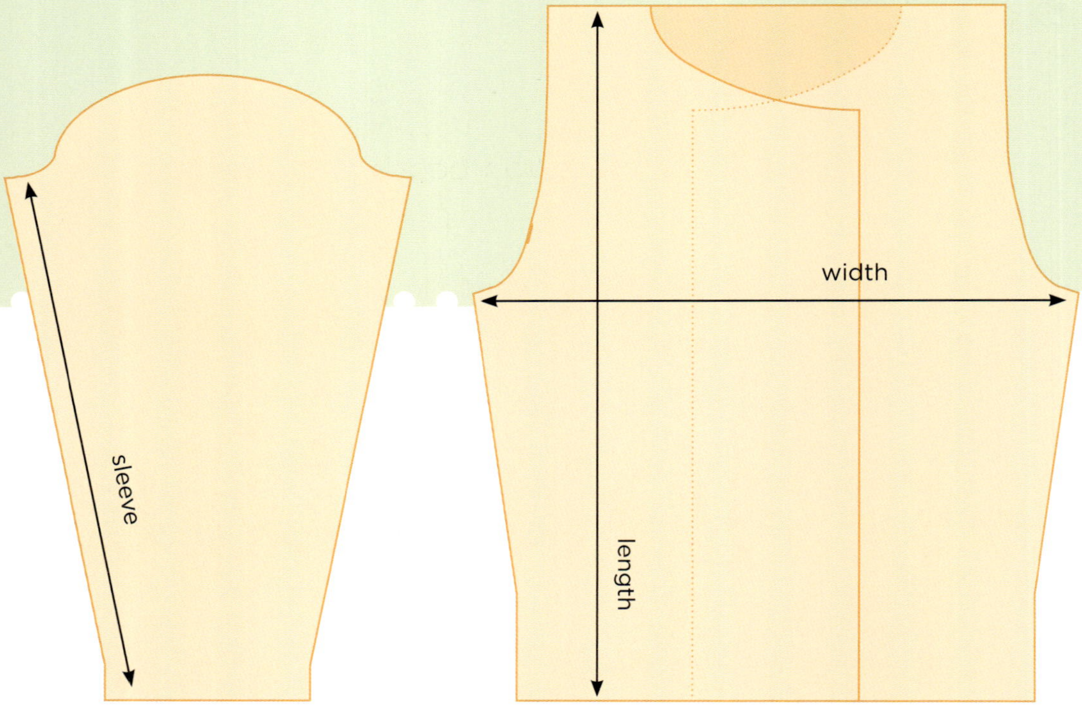

FRONT AND NECK EDGING

Row 1: (RS) Join yarn with a dc in 1st dc of right front edge, * [miss 1 dc, 4 tr in next dc, miss 1 dc, 1 dc in next dc] * 21 (21:22:22: 23:23:24) times up right front edge, miss 1 dc, 4 tr in corner dc, miss 1 dc, 1 dc in next dc, rep from * to * 17 (17:17:18:18:19:19) times around neck edge, miss 1 dc, 4 tr in corner dc, miss 1 dc, 1 dc in next dc, rep from * to * 21 (21:22:22:23:23:24) times down left front edge.

Rows 2 and 4: 1 ch, 1 dc in each st to end.

Row 3: 1 dc in 1st dc, 2 ch, 1 tr in same dc, [2 tr in each dc] to end.

Row 5: 1 dc in 1st dc, 2 ch, [1 tr in each dc] to end, do not turn.

Row 6: (RS) Working from left to right, work 1 dc in each st. Fasten off.

FINISHING

Press according to ball band. Set in sleeves. Taking one st in from each edge, join side and sleeve seams.

Cuff edging

With RS facing join yarn with a dc in sleeve seam and work around edge as given for Row 1 of front and neck edging, then work Row 6 of front and neck edging. Fasten off.

Keep your work clean by storing it in a pillow case.

slip dress

This simple slip of a dress, worked in a combination of trebles and a lacy mesh stitch, uses a silky yarn and has silver teardrop beads around the hem to add extra interest.

By Sue Whiting, from her book *Party Crochet*

Sew the collar to the neck edge using a firm back stitch to avoid the neckline stretching.

INTERMEDIATE

MEASUREMENTS

To fit bust

in.	32	34	36	38	40	42
cm	81	86	91	97	102	107

Actual size, at underarm

in.	32	33¾	35¾	37¾	39¾	41¾
cm	81	86	91	96	101	106

Actual length, from shoulder (approx)

in.	37	37½	37¾	38	38½	39
cm	94	95	96	97	98	99

MATERIALS

- 9 (10: 11: 12: 13: 14) x 50 g balls of Twilleys Silky in black 79
- 2.00 mm crochet hook
- 310 (334: 350: 374: 390: 414) x silver teardrop pearl beads

GAUGE

32 sts and 15 rows to 4 in. (10 cm) measured over treble fabric using 2.00 mm hook. 4 pattern repeats to 4¼ in. (11 cm) and 16 rows to 4 in. (10 cm) measured over mesh pattern using 2.00 mm hook. Change hook size if necessary to obtain this gauge.

ABBREVIATIONS

dc2tog - *insert hook as indicated, yoh and draw loop through, rep from * once more, yoh and draw through all 3 loops on hook

tr2tog - *yoh and insert hook as indicated, yoh and draw loop through, yoh and draw through 2 loops, rep from * once more, yoh and draw through all 3 loops on hook

tr3tog - *yoh and insert hook as indicated, yoh and draw loop through, yoh and draw through 2 loops, rep from * twice more, yoh and draw through all 4 loops on hook.

See also page 51.

Helpful hint. Twilleys Silky is a very slippery yarn and the stitches can easily fall undone. Each time you put your work down, it's a good idea to slip the working loop onto a safety pin to make sure it does not unravel!

BODICE

With 2.00 mm hook, make 260 (276: 292: 308: 324: 340) ch and join with a ss to form a ring.

Foundation round: (RS) 3 ch (counts as first tr), miss ch at base of 3 ch, 1 tr into each ch to end, ss to top of 3 ch at beg of round, turn. 260 (276: 292: 308: 324: 340) sts.

Cont in tr fabric as follows:

Round 1: (WS) 3 ch (counts as 1 tr), miss st at base of 3 ch, 1 tr into each tr to end, ss to top of 3 ch at beg of round, turn.

This round forms tr fabric. (Beg and end of rounds is center back point.)

Work a further 10 rounds in tr fabric, ending with a WS round.

Fasten off.

SHAPE TOP EDGE

Miss first 73 (79: 85: 91: 97: 103) sts of next round, rejoin yarn to next tr with RS facing, 3 ch (counts as first tr), miss tr where yarn was rejoined, 1 tr into each of next 52 (54: 56: 58: 60: 62) tr, tr3tog over next 3 tr, 1 tr into next tr (this is tr before center front point) and turn, leaving rem sts unworked.

Work in tr fabric in **rows** on this set of 55 (57: 59: 61: 63: 65) sts only for first side of top edge.

Next row: 3 ch (counts as first tr), tr3tog over next 3 sts - 2 sts decreased, 1 tr into each tr to last 4 sts, tr3tog over next 3 sts - 2 sts decreased, 1 tr into top of 3 ch at beg of previous row, turn. 51 (53: 55: 57: 59: 61) sts.

Working all decreases as set by last row, dec 2 sts at each end of next 8 (10: 6: 8: 4: 6) rows, ending with a WS row. 19 (13: 31: 25: 43: 37) sts.

Next row: (RS) 3 ch (counts as first tr), tr2tog over next 2 sts - 1 st decreased, 1 tr into each tr to last 4 sts, tr3tog over next 3 sts - 2 sts decreased, 1 tr into top of 3 ch at beg of previous row, turn.

Next row: 3 ch (counts as first tr), tr3tog over next 3 sts - 2 sts decreased, 1 tr into each tr to last 3 sts, tr2tog over next 2 sts - 1 st decreased, 1 tr into top of 3 ch at beg of previous row, turn. 13 (7: 25: 19: 37: 31) sts.

Rep last 2 rows 1 (0: 3: 2: 5: 4) times more, then first of these rows again. 4 sts.

Next row: (WS) 3 ch (does NOT count as st), tr3tog over last 3 sts.

Fasten off.

Return to last complete round worked, with RS facing rejoin yarn to next tr after first side of top edge, 3 ch (counts as first tr), miss tr where yarn was rejoined, tr3tog over next 3 tr, 1 tr into each of next 53 (55: 57: 59: 61: 63) tr and turn, leaving rem sts unworked. 55 (57: 59: 61: 63: 65) sts.

Working all shaping as set by first side, dec 2 sts at center front edge of next 14 (14: 16: 16: 18: 18) rows and at the same time dec 2 sts at side edge of next 9 (11: 7: 9: 5: 7) rows, then 1 st at this edge on foll 5 (3: 9: 7: 13: 11) rows. 4 sts.

Next row: (WS) 3 ch (does NOT count as st), tr3tog over last 3 sts.

Fasten off.

SKIRT

With RS facing and using 2.00 mm hook, rejoin yarn to foundation ch edge of Bodice at center back, 1 ch (does NOT count as st), 1 dc into each foundation ch, ss to first dc, **turn**. 260 (276: 292: 308: 324: 340) sts.

Round 2: (WS) 1 ch (does NOT count as st), 1 dc into each dc to end, ss to first dc, turn.

Round 3: 4 ch (counts as first tr and 1 ch), miss dc at base of 4 ch and next dc, *1 tr into next dc, 1 ch, miss 1 dc, rep from * to end, ss to 3rd of 4 ch at beg of round, turn.

Round 4: 1 ch (does NOT count as st), 1 dc into each ch sp and tr to end, ss to first dc, turn.

Round 5: As round 2.

These 5 rounds complete underbust section.

Helpful Hints

➤ When buying lurex or glittery metallic yarns, make sure they have a polyester base as some materials will tarnish or lose their shine over time.

➤ As the dress will "drop" slightly in wear, it's a good idea to measure the length of the skirt section with it hanging, not laid flat.

Next round: (WS) 1 ch (does NOT count as st), 1 dc into first dc, [5 ch, miss 3 dc, 1 dc into next dc] 8 (7: 8: 8: 9: 8) times, [5 ch, miss 2 dc, 1 dc into next dc] 22 (26: 26: 30: 30: 34) times, [5 ch, miss 3 dc, 1 dc into next dc] 16 (16: 18: 16: 18: 18) times, [5 ch, miss 2 dc, 1 dc into next dc] 22 (26: 26: 30: 30: 34) times, [5 ch, miss 3 dc, 1 dc into next dc] 7 (6: 7: 7: 8: 7) times, 5 ch, miss 3 dc, ss to dc at beg of round, turn. 76 (82: 86: 92: 96: 102) ch sps.

Cont in mesh patt as follows:

Round 1: (RS) 3 ch (counts as first tr), 2 tr into dc at base of 3 ch, *1 dc into next ch sp, 5 ch, miss 1 dc, 1 dc into next ch sp**, 5 tr into next dc, rep from * to end, ending last rep at **, 2 tr into same place as tr at beg of round, ss to top of 3 ch at beg of round. 38 (41: 43: 46: 48: 51) patt reps.

Round 2: 1 ch (does NOT count as st), 1 dc into same place as ss at end of previous round, *5 ch, miss (2 tr and 1 dc), 1 dc into next ch sp**, 5 ch, miss (1 dc and 2 tr), 1 dc into next tr, rep from * to end, ending last rep at **, 2 ch, miss (1 dc and 2 tr), 1 tr into dc at beg of round.

Round 3: 1 ch (does NOT count as st), 1 dc into ch sp partly formed by tr at end of previous round, *5 ch, miss 1 dc, 1 dc into next ch sp, 5 tr into next dc, 1 dc into next ch sp, rep from * to end, replacing dc at end of last rep with ss to first dc.

Round 4: ss across and into center of first ch sp, 1 ch (does NOT count as st), 1 dc into same ch sp, *5 ch, miss (1 dc and 2 tr), 1 dc into next tr, 5 ch, miss (2 tr and 1 dc), 1 dc into next ch sp, rep from * to end, replacing dc at end of last rep with ss to first dc.

These 4 rounds form mesh patt.

Cont in mesh patt until Skirt measures 62 (63: 63: 64: 64: 65) cm, 24½ (24¾: 24¾: 25: 25: 25½) ins, from round 5 of underbust section, ending with patt round 2 or 4. 76 (82: 86: 92: 96: 102) ch sps. Fasten off.

Work hem border

Thread beads onto yarn.

With RS facing, rejoin yarn into one ch sp at center back and cont as follows:

Round 1: 1 ch (does NOT count as st), 1 dc into ch sp where yarn was rejoined, *7 ch, (1 dc, 1 beaded ch and 1 dc) into next ch sp, rep from * to end, replacing dc at end of last rep with ss to first dc.

Round 2: ss along and into center of first ch sp, 1 ch (does NOT count as st), 1 dc into same ch sp, *9 ch, (1 dc, 1 beaded ch and 1 dc) into next ch sp, rep from * to end, replacing dc at end of last rep with ss to first dc.

Round 3: ss along and into center of first ch sp, 1 ch (does NOT count as st), 1 dc into same ch sp, *6 ch, 1 beaded ch, miss beaded ch, ss to next ch, 5 ch, (1 dc, 1 beaded ch and 1 dc) into next ch sp, rep from * to end, replacing dc at end of last rep with ss to first dc.

Fasten off.

FINISHING

Do NOT press.

FRONT NECK EDGING

With RS facing and using 2.00 mm hook, rejoin yarn at fasten-off point at top of left front edge, 1 ch (does NOT count as st), work one row of dc evenly down left front slope, then up right front slope to other fasten-off point, turn.

Next row: (WS) 1 ch (does NOT count as st), 1 dc into each dc to end, working dc2tog at either side of base of center front V neck, turn.

Rep last row once more.

Do NOT fasten off.

ARMHOLE AND BACK EDGING AND SHOULDER STRAPS

With RS facing and using 2.00 mm hook, attach separate length of yarn to beg of last row of Front Neck Edging, make 94 (94: 96: 96: 98: 98) ch (for left shoulder strap) and fasten off.

Helpful Hints

➤ Remember to thread the tie through the underbust casing before working the second tassel end as the beads will be difficult to thread through the crochet.

➤ Teardrop pearl beads come in two varieties - those that have their threading hole across the top narrow end, and those that are drilled from top to bottom. Make sure you buy the kind with the hole at the top!

With RS facing, using 2.00 mm hook and yarn left at end of Front Neck Edging, make 95 (95: 97: 97: 99: 99) ch (for right shoulder strap), 1 dc into 2nd ch from hook, 1 dc into each of next 93 (93: 95: 95: 97: 97) ch, work one row of dc evenly down right armhole edge, across back, then up left armhole edge to ch at top of Front Neck Edging, 1 dc into each ch to end, turn.

Next row: (WS) 1 ch (does NOT count as st), 1 dc into each dc to end, missing dc as required to ensure edging lies flat, turn.

Rep last row once more. Fasten off.

UNDERBUST TIE

Threads 6 beads onto yarn.

Using 2.00 mm hook, make a ch approx 140 (145: 150: 155: 160: 165) cm long and cont as follows: 22 ch, 1 beaded ch, miss beaded ch, 1 dc into each of next 22 ch, 1 ss into next ch, 29 ch, 1 beaded ch, miss beaded ch, 1 dc into each of next 29 ch, 1 ss into same ch as already worked into for first strand of tassel, 16 ch, 1 beaded ch, miss beaded ch, 1 dc into each of next 16 ch, 1 ss into is same ch as already worked into for first and second strands of tassel, 1 dc into each ch to end, break off yarn leaving a very long end but do NOT fasten off. Leave working loop on a safety pin.

Starting and ending at center front, thread Tie in and out of round 3 of underbust section.

Insert hook into working loop and complete tassel at other end of Tie as follows: 22 ch, 1 beaded ch, miss beaded ch, 1 dc into each of next 22 ch, 1 ss into is same ch as last dc was worked into before Tie was threaded through, 29 ch, 1 beaded ch, miss beaded ch, 1 dc into each of next 29 ch, 1 ss into same ch as already worked into for first strand of tassel, 16 ch, 1 beaded ch, miss beaded ch, 1 dc into each of next 16 ch, 1 ss into is same ch as already worked into for first and second strands of tassel.

Fasten off.

Try on dress and adjust length of shoulder straps, attaching them to inside of back edging.

This simple slip of a dress uses a silky yarn and has silver teardrop beads around the hem to add extra interest.

sequin halter neck

The big, bold gold sequins on this simple halter neck top, worked in a smooth and silky yarn, make it a style to really get you noticed. Not one for shrinking violets!

By Sue Whiting, from her book *Party Crochet*

INTERMEDIATE

MEASUREMENTS

To fit bust

in.	32	34	36	38	40	42
cm	81	86	91	97	102	107

Actual size, at underarm

in.	32	34	36	37¾	39¾	41¾
cm	81	86	91	96	101	106

Actual length, from underarm

in.	12¼	12½	12½	13	13	13¼
cm	31	32	32	33	33	34

MATERIALS

- 5 (5: 6: 7: 7: 8) x 50 g balls of Twilleys Silky in beige 101
- 2.00 mm crochet hook
- Approx 2,300 (2,500: 2,600: 2,900: 3,000: 3,300) large gold sequins

GAUGE

32 sts and 20 rows to 4 in. (10 cm) measured over pattern using 2.00 mm hook. Change hook size if necessary to obtain this gauge.

ABBREVIATIONS

dc2tog - *insert hook as indicated, yoh and draw loop through, rep from * once more, yoh and draw through all 3 loops on hook

dc3tog - *insert hook as indicated, yoh and draw loop through, rep from * twice more, yoh and draw through all 4 loops on hook

tr2tog - *yoh and insert hook as indicated, yoh and draw loop through, yoh and draw through 2 loops, rep from * once more, yoh and draw through all 3 loops on hook

tr3tog - *yoh and insert hook as indicated, yoh and draw loop through, yoh and draw through 2 loops, rep from * twice more, yoh and draw through all 4 loops on hook.

See also page 51.

This garment is designed to skim over the body. If you want a tighter fitting garment, make a smaller size.

BACK

With 2.00 mm hook, make 118 (126: 134: 142: 150: 158) ch.

Row 1: (RS) 1 dc into 2nd ch from hook, 1 dc into each ch to end, turn. 117 (125: 133: 141: 149: 157) sts.

Row 2: 1 ch (does NOT count as st), 1 dc into each dc to end, turn.

Rows 3 and 4: As row 2.

Cont in patt as follows:

Row 1: (RS) 3 ch (counts as first tr), miss dc at base of 3 ch, 1 tr into each dc to end, turn.

Row 2: 1 ch (does NOT count as st), 1 dc into each of first 2 tr, *1 sequinned dc into next tr, 1 dc into each of next 3 tr, rep from * to last 3 sts, 1 sequinned dc into next tr, 1 dc into each of last 2 sts, working last dc into top of 3 ch at beg of previous row, turn.

Row 3: As row 1.

Row 4: 1 ch (does NOT count as st), 1 dc into each of first 4 tr, *1 sequinned dc into next tr, 1 dc into each of next 3 tr, rep from * to last 5 sts, 1 sequinned dc into next tr, 1 dc into each of last 4 sts, working last dc into top of 3 ch at beg of previous row, turn.

These 4 rows form patt.

Cont in patt for a further 2 rows, ending with a WS row.

Dec row: (RS) 3 ch (counts as first tr), miss dc at base of 3 ch, tr2tog over

Make sure the sequins have the hole near one edge, not in the center as otherwise they will not lie flat.

Helpful hint. When working the top edge shaping, remember not to place any sequins on the actual edge stitches of the rows as these edge sequins will get in the way when working the edgings.

next 2 dc - 1 st decreased, 1 tr into each dc to last 3 dc, tr2tog over next 2 dc - 1 st decreased, 1 tr into last dc, turn.

Working all decreases as set by last row, dec 1 st at each end of every foll 4th row until 109 (117: 125: 133: 141: 149) sts rem.

Work 3 rows, ending with a WS row.

Inc row: (RS) 3 ch (counts as first tr), miss dc at base of 3 ch, 2 tr into next dc - 1 st increased, 1 tr into each dc to last 2 dc, 2 tr into next dc - 1 st increased, 1 tr into last dc, turn.

Working all increases as set by last row, inc 1 st at each end of every foll 4th row until there are 129 (137: 145: 153: 161: 169) sts, taking inc sts into patt.

Work a further 1 (3: 3: 5: 5: 7) rows, ending with a WS row.**

Fasten off.

FRONT

Work as given for Back to **.

SHAPE ARMHOLES

Next row: (RS) ss across and into 7th (9th: 11th: 13th: 15th: 17th) st, 3 ch (counts as first tr), miss dc at base of 3 ch, 1 tr into each dc to last 6 (8: 10: 12: 14: 16) dc and turn, leaving rem sts unworked. 117 (121: 125: 129: 133: 137) sts.

Next row: 1 ch (does NOT count as st), dc2tog over first 2 tr - 1 st decreased, patt to last 2 sts, dc2tog over last 2 sts - 1 st decreased, turn. 115 (119: 123: 127: 131: 135) sts.

Working all decreases as set by last row and Back side seam shaping, dec 1 st at each end of next 2 rows, ending with a WS row. 111 (115: 119: 123: 127: 131) sts.

SHAPE NECK

Next row: (RS) 3 ch (counts as first tr), miss dc at base of 3 ch, tr2tog over next 2 dc - 1 st decreased, 1 tr into each of next 48 (50: 52: 54: 56: 58) dc, tr3tog over next 3 dc - 2 sts decreased, 1 tr into next dc and turn, leaving rem sts unworked. 52 (54: 56: 58: 60: 62) sts.

Next row: 1 ch (does NOT count as st), dc3tog over first 3 sts - 2 sts decreased, patt to last 2 sts, dc2tog over last 2 sts - 1 st decreased, turn. 49 (51: 53: 55: 57: 59) sts.

Working all decreases as now set, dec 2 sts at neck edge and 1 st at armhole edge of next 15 (15: 16: 17: 17: 18) rows, ending with a RS (RS: WS: RS: RS: WS) row. 4 (6: 5: 4: 6: 5) sts.

For 1st, 2nd, 4th and 5th sizes

Next row: (WS) 1 ch (does NOT count as st), [dc2tog over next 2 sts] 2 (0: 2: 0) times, [dc3tog over next 3 sts] 0 (2: 0: 2) times. 2 sts.

For 3rd and 4th sizes

Next row: (RS) 3 ch (does NOT count as st), tr3tog over next 3 sts, 1 tr into last dc. 2 sts.

All sizes

Fasten off.

Return to last complete row worked, miss center dc, rejoin yarn to next dc with RS facing, 3 ch (counts as first tr), miss dc at base of 3 ch, tr3tog over next 3 dc - 2 sts decreased, 1 tr into each dc to last 3 dc, tr2tog over next 2 dc - 1 st decreased, 1 tr into last dc, turn. 52 (54: 56: 58: 60: 62) sts. Complete to match first side, reversing shaping.

Helpful hint. The sequins will tend to fold themselves out of position as this top is made. Once finished and in wear, gently smooth them all downward to create the shimmery fish-scale effect.

FINISHING

Do NOT press.
Join side seams.

Front Neck Border

With RS facing and 2.00 mm hook, rejoin yarn at left front fasten-off point, 1 ch (does NOT count as st), work in dc down left front slope, then up right front slope to right front fasten-off point, working dc2tog either side of base of V neck, turn.

Next row: 1 ch (does NOT count as st), 1 dc into each dc to end, working dc2tog either side of base of V neck, turn.

Rep last row twice more.

Fasten off.

Back and Armhole Borders and Ties

With 2.00 mm hook, make 150 ch, with RS facing and starting at top of Front Neck Border, work in dc evenly down right front armhole edge, across top of Back, then up left front armhole edge to top of other end of Front Neck Border, 151 ch, turn.

Next row: (WS) 1 dc into 2nd ch from hook, 1 dc into each ch and dc to end, turn.

Next row: 1 ch (does NOT count as st), 1 dc into each dc to end, turn.

Rep last row once more.

Fasten off.

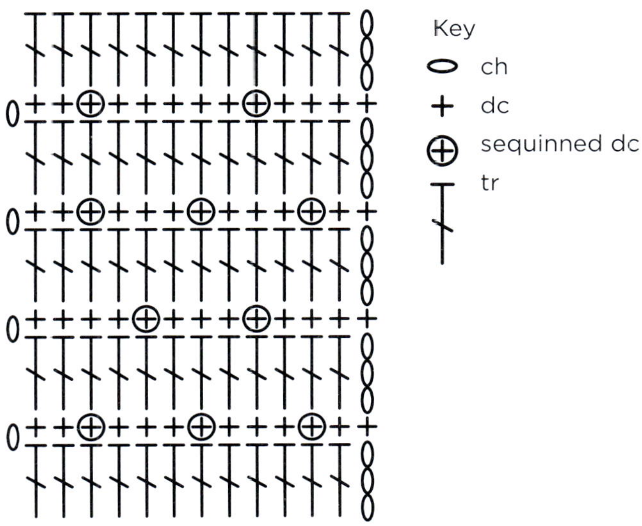

leaf motif poncho

There are just four rounds to each of the leaf motif blocks that are joined in a square to make this dramatic poncho.

By Melody Griffiths, from her book *Simple Stylish Crochet*

INTERMEDIATE

MEASUREMENTS

One size

Actual width
40 in. (102 cm)

Actual length (from shoulder to point)
28¼ in. (72 cm)

MATERIALS

- 13 x 50 g balls of Patons Diploma Gold DK in Apple Green 06125
- 4.00 mm crochet hook

GAUGE

One leaf block measures 5 × 5 in. (12.5 × 12.5 cm) when pressed, using 4.00 mm hook. Change hook size if necessary to obtain this gauge.

ABBREVIATIONS

quadtr - quadruple treble
quintr - quintuple treble
See also page 51.

➤ Instructions are given for making and joining all of the leaf motif blocks, then working all the filler motifs. If you prefer, you could work the filler motifs as you join the blocks.

PONCHO

LEAF MOTIF BLOCK

Make 8 ch, ss in 1st ch to form a ring.

Round 1: (RS) 7 ch, [2 dc in ring, 6 ch] 7 times, 2 dc in ring, ss in 1st ch, ss in each of next 2 ch.

Round 2: 1 ch, 2 dc in 1st 7-ch loop, [16 ch, miss next 6-ch loop, 3 dc in next 6-ch loop] 3 times, 16 ch, 1 dc in 1st 6-ch loop, ss in 1st dc.

Round 3: Work [2 dc, 2 htr, 2 tr, 2 dtr, 2 trtr, 2 quadtr, 1 quintr, 2 quadtr, 2 trtr, 2 dtr, 2 tr, 2 htr, 2 dc] in each 16-ch loop.

Round 4: * Ss in each of next 2 dc, [4 ch, ss in each of next 2 sts] 11 times, ss in last dc of leaf, rep from * 3 more times, ss in 1st ss.

Fasten off.

1ST LINE OF BLOCKS, SECOND MOTIF

Work as first motif to Round 4.

Round 4: * Ss in each of next 2 dc, [4 ch, ss in each of next 2 sts] 11 times, ss in last dc of leaf, rep from * once more, ** ss in each of next 2 dc, [4 ch, ss in each of next 2 sts] 5 times, with WS together join to 6th 4-ch loop at point of leaf of previous motif by working 2 ch, dc in 4-ch loop, 2 ch, ss in each of next 2 sts, [4 ch, ss in each of next 2 sts] 5 times, ss in last dc of leaf, rep from ** once more, joining in 4-ch loop of next leaf of previous motif, ss in 1st ss. Fasten off.

Continue making and joining blocks in this way until 1st line of 8 blocks has been completed.

2ND AND 3RD LINES OF BLOCKS

Join 8 blocks in the same way but linking blocks to 4-ch loops of previous row as well as to each other.

4TH AND 5TH LINES OF BLOCKS

Join 3 blocks, omit center two blocks, join 3 blocks.

6TH, 7TH, AND 8TH LINES OF BLOCKS

Join as 2nd line of blocks.

BLOCK FILLER MOTIFS

Worked into center three 4-ch sps of each of 4 leaves of adjacent blocks.

Loop yarn around first finger to make a ring.

Round 1: (RS) 1 ch, 12 dc in ring, pull end to close ring, ss in 1st dc.

Round 2: 2 ch, * 1 dc in 2nd 4-ch sp of 1st leaf, [2 ch, ss in next dc of 1st round, 2 ch, 1 dc in next 4-ch sp] twice, 2 ch, ss in next dc of 1st round, rep from * working into center three 4-ch sps of each of next 3 leaves, ending ss in 1st dc of 1st round. Fasten off.

Work a filler motif in each space between blocks.

This poncho is made from 4-leaf motifs joined to form a square with the four motifs at the center omitted to make the neck hole.

Helpful hint. You can work over the end of the 8-ch ring at the center of the leaf motif block for a few stitches, then just snip it off but the end of each filler motif should be thoroughly darned in before trimming.

NECK FILLER MOTIFS

Work in same way as block filler motif but make only 9 dc in ring on 1st round and join into 2 leaves of motif only.

NECKBAND

With RS facing, join yarn in a joined 4-ch sp at one corner of neck.

Round 1: (RS) 1 ch, [2 dc in 1st ch sp of block, 3 dc in each of next 3 ch sps, 1 dc in each of next 3 dc of filler motif, 3 dc in each of next 3 ch sps, 2 dc in foll ch sp] 8 times, ss in 1st dc. [200 sts.] Missing 1st dc, 2 dc at each corner and last dc on each round, work 7 rounds dc. [144 sts.] Fasten off.

EDGING

With RS facing, join yarn in joined 4-ch sp of 2nd block along from one corner of outer edge of poncho.

Round 1: (RS) 1 ch, * [1 dc in joined 4-ch sp, 4 dc in each of next four 4-ch sps, 1 dc in each of 2 foll 4-ch sps, 4 dc in each of next four 4-ch sps, 1 dc in joined 4-ch sp] 6 times, 1 dc in joined 4-ch sp, 4 dc in each of next four 4-ch sps, 1 dc in each of 2 foll

Helpful hint. Using different height stitches makes Round 3 of the motif grow really quickly. Here's a reminder of how many times to take the yarn around the hook before inserting the hook to work the stitches: dc = no times, htr = once but pull through all loops first time; tr = once; dtr = twice, trtr = 3 times; quadtr = 4 times, quintr = 5 times.

Save finishing time by darning in the ends as you join motifs.

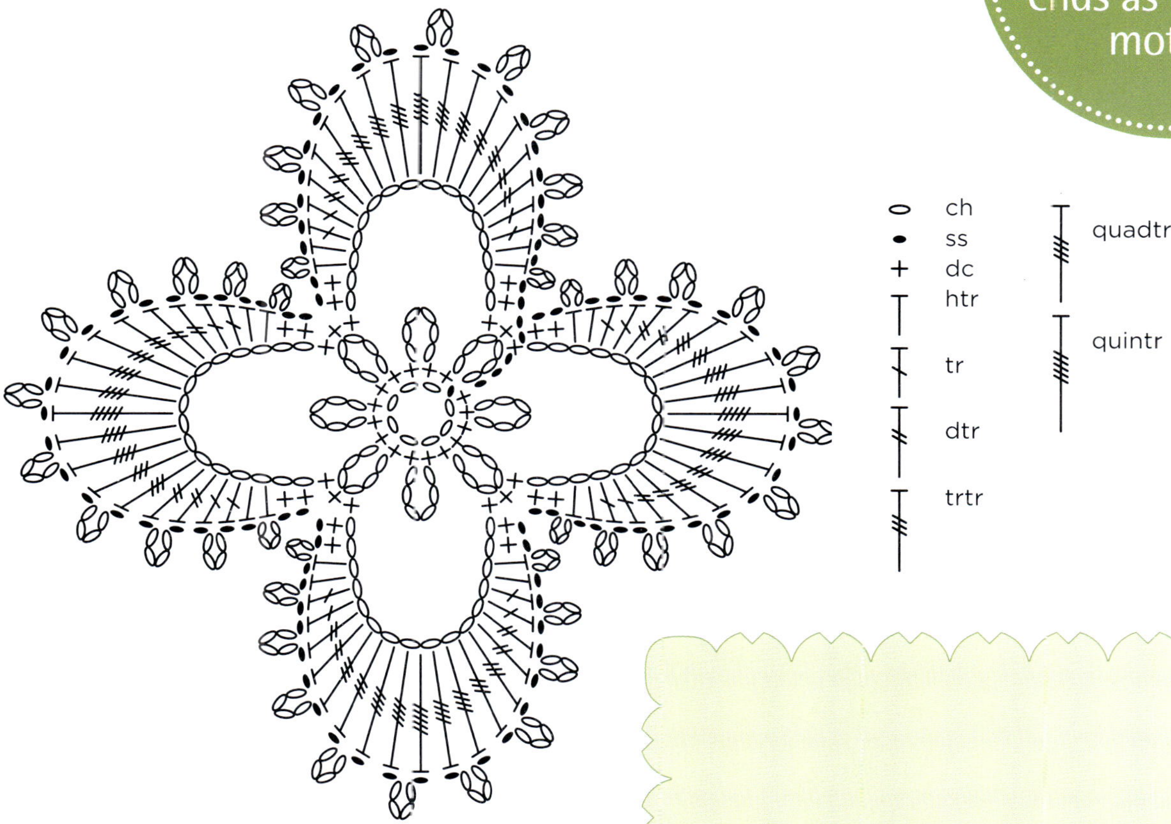

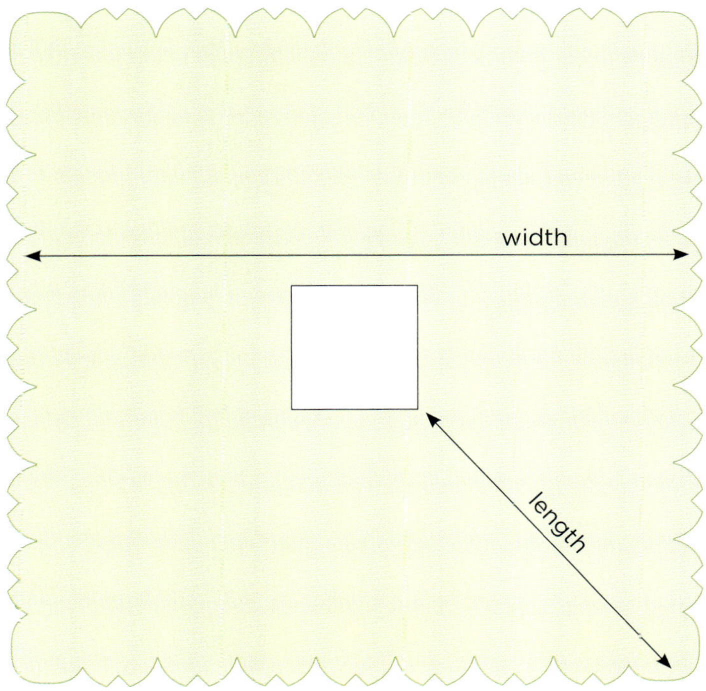

4-ch sps, 4 dc in each of next four 4-ch sps, 7 dc in corner 4-ch sp, 4 dc in each of next four 4-ch sps, 1 dc in each of 2 foll 4-ch sps, 4 dc in each of next four 4-ch sps, 1 dc in joined 4-ch sp, rep from * 3 more times, ss in 1st dc. Fasten off.

FINISHING

Press according to ball band. Darn in ends.

tunic with lace borders

The main body and sleeves of this lightweight cotton tunic are worked in simple double crochet stitches with an attractive lacy border on the front, back, and sleeves. Wear this sweater with a belt over jeans or a skirt or as a casual beach cover-up.

By Sue Whiting and Hilary Mackin, from their book *Big Book of Weekend Crochet*

ADVANCED

MEASUREMENTS

To fit bust

in.	32–34	36	38	40–42
cm	81–86	91	97	102–107

Actual width

in.	38	40	43½	46
cm	95	102	110	117

Length from shoulder

in.	27	27½	28½	28½
cm	68	70	72	72

Sleeve seam

18 in. (46 cm)

MATERIALS

- 12 (13:14:15) x 50 g (1¾ oz.) balls of Rowan 4-ply Cotton in Bluebell 136
- C/2 (2.75 mm) and D/3 (3.25 mm) crochet hooks

GAUGE

22 sts and 13 rows to 4 in. (10 cm) measured over double crochet pattern, using C/2 (2.75 mm) crochet hook. Change hook size, if necessary, to obtain this gauge.

ABBREVIATIONS

inc - increase at beg of row by working ch 3, 1 dc into same st; inc at end of row by working 2 dc into the same st.
bobble - leaving last loop of each st on hook, work 4 dc into next st, yoh and draw through all 5 loops.
dc3tog - leaving last loop of each st on hook, work 1 dc into each of next 3 dc, yoh and draw through all 4 loops to dec 2 sts.
sc2tog - [insert hook in next st, yoh and draw loop through] twice, yoh and draw through all 3 loops to dec 1 st.
See also page 51.

➤ Figures in parentheses refer to the larger sizes; where only one set of figures is given, this refers to all sizes.

SWEATER

BACK AND FRONT (both alike)

Using smaller hook, ch 106 (114:122:130).

HEM EDGE

Foundation row (WS) 1 sc into 2nd ch from hook, 1 sc into each ch to end, turn. 105 (113:121:129) sts.

Next row Ch 1 (counts as 1 sc), 1 sc in each sc, 1 sc in tch, turn.

Rep last row 2 more times.

BORDER PATTERN

Change to larger hook. Cont in border patt as follows:

Row 1 (WS) Ch 4 (counts as 1 dc, 1 ch), skip the next st, 1 bobble into next st, ch 1, skip 1 st, 1 dc into next st, *ch 1, skip 1 st, 1 bobble into next st, ch 1, skip 1 st, 1 dc into next st; rep from * to end, turn.

Row 2 Ch 2 (counts as first hdc), work 1 hdc into each dc, ch sp, and bobble to end, ending 1 hdc into last ch sp, 1 hdc into 3rd of 4 ch, turn.

Row 3 Ch 1, 1 sc into each of first 3 sc, *ch 5, skip 3 sc, 1 sc into each of next 5 sc; rep from * to end omitting 2 sc at end of last rep, turn.

Row 4 Ch 1, 1 sc into each of first 2 sc, *ch 3, 1 sc into 5-ch arch, ch 3, skip 1 sc, 1 sc into each of next 3 sc; rep from * to end, omitting 1 sc at end of last rep, turn.

The attractive lacy border adds a special touch.

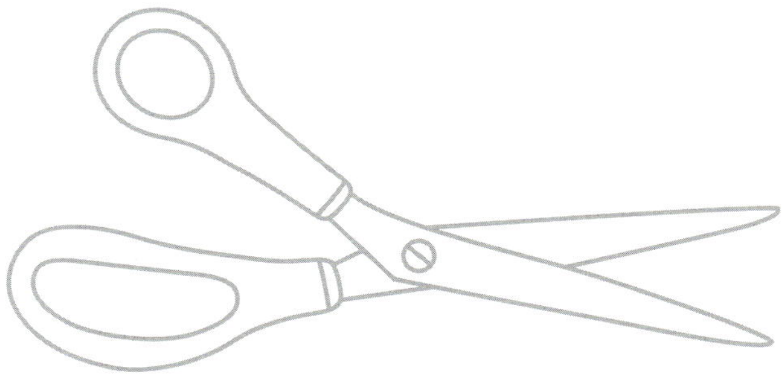

Row 5 Ch 1, 1 sc into first sc, *ch 3, 1 sc into next 3-ch arch, 1 sc into next sc, 1 sc into next 3-ch arch, ch 3, skip 1 sc, 1 sc into next sc; rep from * to end, turn.

Row 6 Ch 5 (count as 1 dc, 2 ch), 1 sc into next 3-ch arch, 1 sc into each of next 3 sc, 1 sc into next 3-ch arch, *ch 5, 1 sc into next 3-ch arch, 1 sc into each of next 3 sc, 1 sc into next 3-ch arch; rep from * to last sc, ch 2, 1 dc into last sc, turn.

Row 7 Ch 1, 1 sc into first dc, *ch 3, skip 1 sc, 1 sc into each of next 3 sc, ch 3, 1 sc into next 5-ch arch; rep from * to end placing last sc into 3rd of 5 ch at beg of previous row, turn.

Row 8 Ch 1, 1 sc into first sc, *1 sc into next 3-ch arch, ch 3, skip 1 sc, 1 sc into next sc, ch 3, 1 sc into next 3-ch arch, 1 sc into next sc; rep from * to end, turn.

Row 9 Ch 1, 1 sc into each of first 2 sc, *1 sc into next 3-ch arch, ch 3, 1 sc into next 3-ch arch, 1 sc into each of next 3 sc; rep from * to end omitting 1 sc at end of last rep, turn.

Row 10 Ch 2 (count as first hdc), 1 hdc into each of next 2 sc, *3 hdc into next 3-ch arch, 1 hdc into each of next 5 sc; rep from * to end omitting 2 sc at end of last rep, turn.

Row 11 Ch 4 (count as 1 dc, ch 1), skip next hdc, 1 bobble into next hdc, ch 1, skip 1 hdc, 1 dc into next hdc, *ch 1, skip 1 hdc, 1 bobble into next hdc, ch 1, skip 1 hdc, 1 dc into next hdc; rep from * to end, turn.

Row 12 As Row 2. 105 (113:121:129) sts.

Rep Rows 1–12 twice more.

These 36 rows complete border.

Change to smaller hook. Cont in main patt as follows:

Next row Ch 3 (counts as 1 dc), 1 dc in each st ending 1 dc in tch, turn.

Rep this row throughout until work measures 25 (26:27:27) in. (64 [66:68:68] cm) from beg.

SHAPE NECK

Row 1 Ch 3 (counts as 1 dc), 1 dc in each of next 39 (41:43:45) dc, turn and work on these 40 (42:44:46) sts for the first side.

Row 2 Ch 3 (counts as 1 dc), dc3tog, 1 dc in each dc ending 1 dc in tch, turn.

Row 3 Ch 3 (counts as 1 dc), 1 dc in each dc to last 4 sts, dc3tog, 1 dc in tch, turn.

Rep the last 2 rows once more, then Row 2 again. 30 (32:34:36) sts.

Leave the center 25 (29:33:37) sts, rejoin yarn to next st, ch 3 (counts as 1 dc), 1 dc in each dc ending 1 dc in tch, turn.

Complete to match first side, reversing shapings.

SLEEVES

Using smaller hook, ch 58 (66:66:74).

HEM EDGE

Foundation row 1 sc into 2nd ch from hook, 1 sc in each ch to end. 57 (65:65:73) sts.

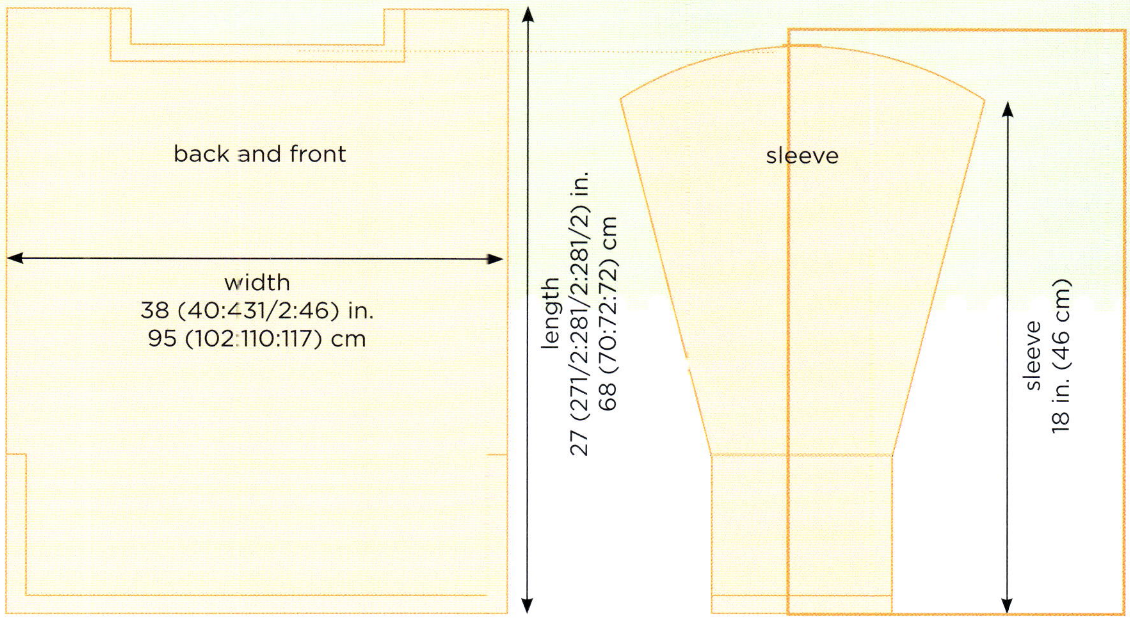

Next row Ch 1 (counts as 1 sc), 1 sc in each sc, ending 1 sc in tch, turn.

Rep the last row 2 more times.

BORDER PATTERN

Change to larger hook. Work 36 rows in border patt as given for Back.

Change to smaller hook. Cont in main patt as follows:

Next row Ch 3 (counts as 1 dc), 1 dc in each st ending 1 dc in tch, turn.

Rep this row throughout, inc 1 st at each end of the next 8 rows. 73 (81:81:89) sts.

[Work 1 row, then inc 1 st at each end of next 2 rows] 5 times. 93 (101:101:109) sts.

Cont straight until Sleeve measures 18 in. (46 cm) from beg.

SHAPE TOP

Next row Ss across and into the 11th (12th:12th:13th) st, ch 3 (counts as 1 dc), 1 dc in each st to the last 10 (11:11:12) sts, turn.

Rep last row 3 more times. 13 sts. Fasten off.

NECKBAND

Join shoulders.

With RS facing and using smaller hook, rejoin yarn to one shoulder. Ch 1 (counts as 1 sc), work in sc evenly around neck edge so that there is a multiple of 4 sts, ss to 1 ch at beg of round, turn.

Next round Ch 4 (counts as 1 dc and 1 ch), skip next sc, *1 bobble into next sc, ch 1, skip next sc, 1 dc in next sc, ch 1, skip next sc; rep from * omitting 1 dc and ch on the last rep, ss to 3rd of 4 ch, turn.

Next round Ch 1 (counts as 1 sc), 1 sc in each dc, ch sp, and bobble, ss to 1 ch. Fasten off.

FINISHING

Mark positions 8½ (9½:9½:10¼) in. (22 [24:24:26] cm) down from each side of shoulder seam. Fold sleeves in half lengthwise, and placing center point at shoulder seams, sew between markers on back and front.

Join sleeve seams. Starting at Row 34 of border, join side seams to underarms. Weave in yarn ends.

SIDE SLITS

With RS facing and using smaller hook, rejoin yarn at lower corner of Right Front.

Row 1 Ch 1 (counts as 1 sc), work in sc along one side of the slit, 1 sc into seam, and mark this st, work same number of sc along other side slit, turn.

Row 2 Ch 1 (counts as 1 sc), work 1 sc in each sc to within 2 sts of marked st, sc2tog, 1 sc in marked st, sc2tog, 1 sc in each st to end, turn.

Rows 3 and 4 As Row 2. Fasten off. Repeat for second slit. Weave in yarn ends.

wraparound cardigan

This wraparound cardigan can be worn for many different occasions; pair it with your favorite jeans for a casual look, wear it over a turtleneck with a long skirt, or use it as a topper with a dress for evening.

By Sue Whiting and Hilary Mackin, from their book *Big Book of Weekend Crochet*

ADVANCED

MEASUREMENTS

To fit bust

in.	32–34	36–38	40–42
cm	81–86	91–97	102–107

Actual width

in.	34½	40	43¼
cm	87	101	110

Length from shoulder

in.	23	23½	24½
cm	58	60	62

Sleeve seam

in.	17½	18	18½
cm	45	46	47

MATERIALS

- 8 (9:10) × 100 g (3½ oz.) balls of Sirdar Cotton DK in Cream 021
- E/4 (3.50 mm) crochet hook

GAUGE

18 sts and 9 rows to 4 in. (10 cm) measured over pattern using E/4 (3.50 mm) crochet hook. Change hook size, if necessary, to obtain this gauge.

ABBREVIATIONS

dc2(3)tog - leaving last loop of each st on hook, work 1 dc into each of next 2 (3) sts, yoh and draw through rem 3 (4) loops on hook, to dec 1 (2) sts.
See also page 51.

➤ Figures in parentheses refer to the larger sizes; where only one set of figures is given, this refers to all sizes.
➤ When decreasing over filet patt (1dc, ch 1, skip next st, 1dc into next st), work a dc into ch sp to work dc3tog.

TOP

BACK

Ch 80 (92:100).

Foundation row 1 sc into 3rd ch from hook, 1 sc into each ch to end, turn, 79 (91:99) sts.

Row 1 Ch 1 (counts as first sc), 1 sc into each st to end, turn.

Rows 2 and 3 As Row 1. Cont in patt:

Next row (RS) Ch 3 (counts as first dc), 1 dc into each of next 2 sts, *ch 1, skip next st, 1 dc into each of next 3 sts, rep from * to end, turn.

Rep the last row throughout. **

Work another 31 rows.

SHAPE ARMHOLES

Next row Ss into each of the first 6 (8:9) sts, ch 3, patt to last 5 (7:8) sts, turn. 69 (77:83) sts.

Next row Dc2tog, patt to last 2 sts, dc2tog.

Rep last row 1 (2:3) more times. 65 (71:75) sts.

Work straight for another 15 (16:17) rows.

SHAPE SHOULDERS

Next row Ss into each of first 10 (11:12) sts, ch 3, patt to 9 (10:11) sts, turn.

Next row Ss into each of first 11 (12:13) sts, ch 3, patt to last 10 (11:12) sts.

Fasten off. 27 (29:29) sts.

LEFT FRONT

Work as given for Back to **. 79 (91:99) sts.

Work another 12 rows.

SHAPE FRONT

Row 1 (WS) Dc3tog, patt to end, turn.

Row 2 Patt to last 3 sts, dc3tog, turn, 75 (87:95) sts.

Rep Rows 1 and 2 eight more times, then work Row 1 again. 41 (53:61) sts.

SHAPE ARMHOLE

Next row Ss into each of first 6 (8:9) sts, ch 3, patt to last 3 sts, dc3tog, turn. 34(44:51) sts.

Next row Dc3tog, patt to last 2 sts, dc2tog, turn. 31 (41:48) sts.

This wraparound cardigan can be worn for many different occasions.

1st size only

Next row Dc2tog, patt to last 2 sts, dc2tog, turn. 29 sts. Keeping armhole edge straight, cont to dec 1 st at front edge on next 10 rows. 19 sts.

2nd and 3rd sizes only

Next row Dc2tog, patt to last 3 sts, dc3tog, turn. 38 (45) sts.

Next row Dc3tog, patt to last 2 sts, dc2tog, turn. 35 (42) sts.

Next row Dc0(2)tog, patt to last 3 sts, dc3tog, turn. 33 (39) sts.

Keeping armhole edge straight, cont to dec 2 (2) sts at front edge on next 3 (7) rows. 27 (25) sts. Dec 1 st at front edge on next 6 (2) rows.

All sizes

19 (21:23) sts. Work 5 (6:8) rows straight.

SHAPE SHOULDER

Next row Ss into each of first 10 (11:12) sts, patt to end.

Fasten off. 10 (11:12) sts.

RIGHT FRONT

Work as given for Left Front–the patt is reversible.

SLEEVES (make 2)

Ch 48 (52:56).

Foundation row 1 sc into 3rd ch from hook, 1 sc into each ch to end, turn. 47 (51:55) sts.

Rows 1–3 As given for Back.

Cont in patt as Back, inc 1 st at each end of 3rd and every foll 4th row until there are 65 (69:73) sts, working inc sts into patt. Patt straight until Sleeve measures 17½ (18:18½) in. (45 [46:47] cm).

SHAPE TOP

Next row Ss into each of first 6 (8:9) sts, patt to last 5 (7:8) sts, turn. 55 (55:57) sts.

Next row Dc3tog, patt to last 3 sts, dc3tog. 51 (51:53) sts.

Rep the last row 9 (8:8) more times. 15 (19:21) sts.

2nd and 3rd sizes only

Next row Dc2tog, patt to last 2 sts, dc2tog, turn.

Rep last row 2 (3) times. 13 sts.

All sizes

Fasten off. Weave in yarn ends.

FRONT EDGING

Join shoulder seams.

With RS facing , join yarn at hem edge on Right Front.

Row 1 Ch 1, work in sc evenly around front edges to hem edge on Left Front,

working a multiple of 2 sts plus 1, turn.

Row 2 Ch 1 (counts as 1 sc), 1 sc in each st to end, turn.

Row 3 Ch 1 (counts as 1 sc), *ch 3, skip next st, 1 sc into next st; rep from * to end. Fasten off. Weave in yarn ends.

TIES

Ch 5.

Next row 1 sc into 2nd ch from hook, 1 sc in each of 3 ch, turn. 4 sts.

Next row Ch 1 (counts as 1 sc), 1 sc in each st to end, turn.

Rep the last row until tie measures approximately 16 in. (40 cm). Fasten off. This will be the right tie. For the left tie, work as given above until tie measures approximately 32 in. (81 cm).

FINISHING

Sew ties to fronts, under edging, and level with last 2 rows below front shaping. Set in sleeves. Join side seams, leaving 2 rows open on right side seam in line with ties for tie to go through. Join sleeve seams.

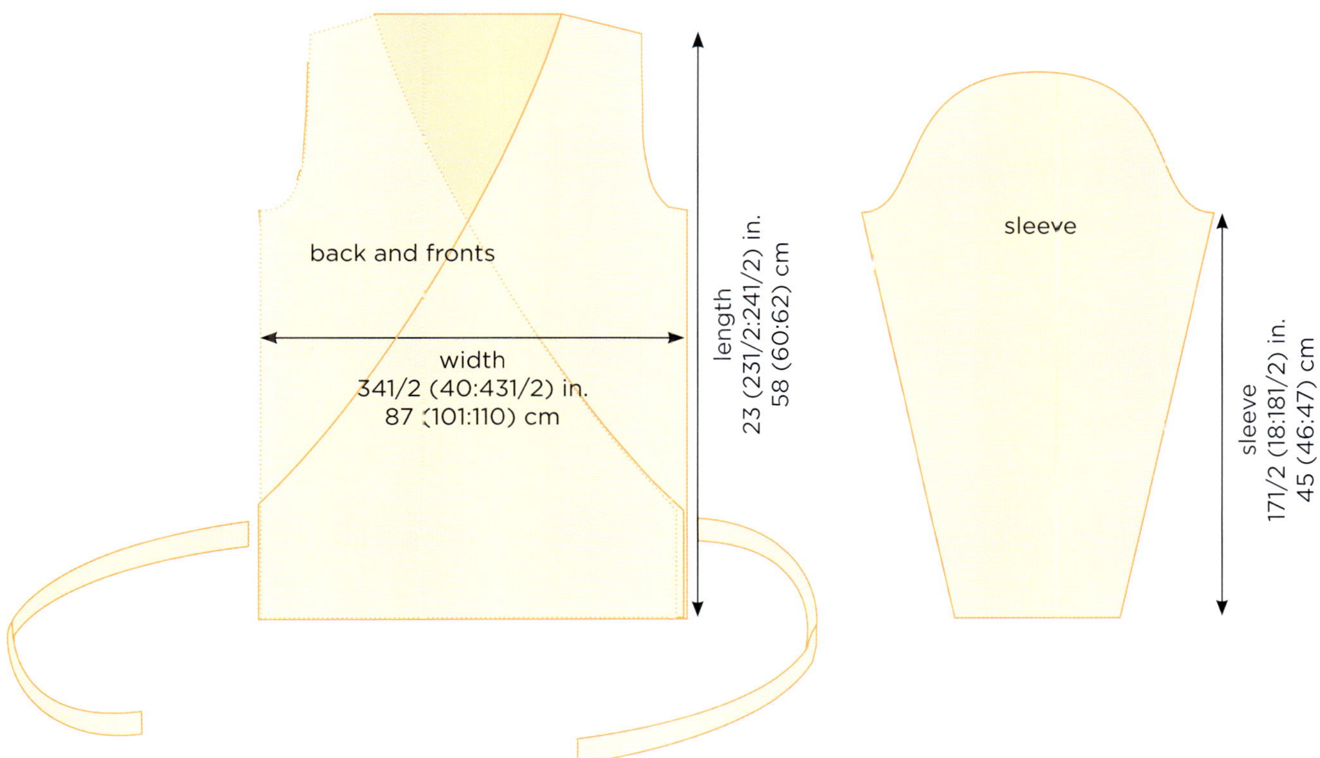

Contributors

MELODY GRIFFITHS

Melody Griffiths commissioned and designed garments and accessories for women's magazines and worldwide yarn manufacturers for over 20 years. As well as designing, she worked as a knitting editor and is the author of many knitting and crochet books.

HILARY MACKIN

Hilary Mackin began a career in nursing, moved to banking, and then took a full-time fashion and textiles course, specializing in knitting. Her distinction in this course led her to begin designing her own knitwear, and since then she has never looked back. She now designs regularly for all the major magazines. She is constantly in demand and as she comments, "Still knitting, still loving it."

VAL PIERCE

Val Pierce's passion for knitting began when her father taught her to knit at the age of five. Later in life she began home knitting for yarn manufacturers, and since then she has made a huge range of items, from evening dresses to teddy bears. She later began designing items of her own, and before long her designs were appearing in knitting and crochet magazines. She also teaches knitting and crochet to both adults and children.

SUE WHITING

Sue Whiting is a professional needlecraft design consultant and author who works with several textile companies to produce brochures, booklets, and promotional materials. Her clients include Jaeger and Rowan Handknitting. She trained at the London School of Fashion and has worked with numerous magazines and publishers on all aspects of needlework.

KNITTING & CROCHET shopping guide | free shipping on all orders!*

Love... Knitting
$16.99 • #5942L

Lace Collection for Knitting
$17.99 • #DO5418

Hip Knitting
$12.99 • #DO5397

Knitting & Crochet
$9.95 • #6837

Arm Knitting
$9.99 • #DO5480

Finger Knitting
$9.99 • #DO5481

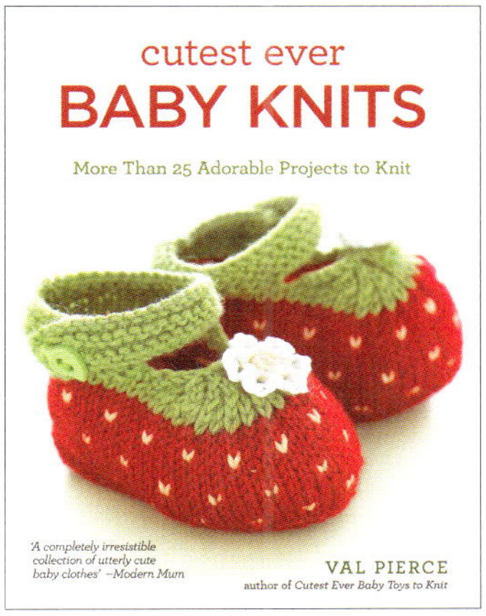

Cutest Ever Baby Knits
$14.99 • #00167

Cutest Ever Toddler Knits
$19.95 • #1006

Party Knits
$16.99 • #01034

ORDER TODAY!

800-457-9112 · www.D-Originals.com